THE DECCAN RYOTS
AND THEIR
LAND TENURE.

THE DECCAN RYOTS

AND THEIR

LAND TENURE.

BY

H. GREEN,

PROFESSOR OF LITERATURE AT POONAH COLLEGE.

ISBN: 978-93-5128-455-0(HB)

First Published in 1852
Indian Reprint in 2017

Published by

Kalpaz Publications
C-30, Satyawati Nagar,
Delhi – 110052
E-mail: kalpaz@hotmail.com
Website: kalpazpublications.com
Ph.: +91-9212142040

PREFACE.

This pamphlet is a reprint of a series of articles which appeared in the *Bombay Gazette*, in the months of June, July, and August, 1852.

The subject of Land Tenures, which has always excited great attention in India, has recently also been forced into some prominence at home by the agitation of the Tenant Right League in Ireland; and it was thought that an account of a Tenure in some respects resembling the one which it is sought to obtain through that agitation, and which has been voluntarily granted to the peasantry of a portion of the Bombay Presidency, and is about, with all practicable speed, to be extended to the remainder, might prove interesting in England as well as in India.

It will be seen that, in the course of the inquiry, the writer's means of information, (which are for the most part indicated in the last article,) grew more extensive, and that he speaks, therefore, on one or two points with more confidence and decision in the latter than in the former portion of the pamphlet. There is also a certain assumption of identity with the Editor of the spirited and ably-conducted Journal in which the articles originally appeared, which, now that they are published in a separate form, the writer of course begs to disclaim.

Poonah, September, 1852.

THE DECCAN RYOTS AND THEIR LAND TENURE.

SELECTIONS FROM THE BOMBAY RECORDS, No. I., COMPRISING Captain Wingate's Report on Survey and Assessment for Khandeish, and the Instructions issued on the subject by Government. 1852.

OFFICIAL CORRESPONDENCE ON THE SYSTEM OF REVENUE SURVEY AND ASSESSMENT OF THE BOMBAY PRESIDENCY. 1850.

REPORT ON THE INTRODUCTORY ASSESSMENT OF TWO TURUFS IN TALOOKA CHANDORE. 1840.

WE beg to welcome very cordially the accession of the Bombay Government to the Editorial Corps of Bombay. Selections from the records, if at all judiciously made, ought to form a perfectly readable and very instructive periodical, and no moderately good government can have anything to fear from the publication, from time to time, of the best of the papers sent in to it by its servants.

A first appearance, whatever its intrinsic merits, may usually look to be courteously received ; but the Bombay Government's No. I., we are bound to say, does not need our forbearance, and can perfectly well afford to stand on its own merits,—the only criticism to which it is open being that the amount of matter selected is wonderfully small.

On the subject of Revenue Surveys and Assessments, we pretend to no very extensive personal knowledge, but from all that we have been able to collect, we are inclined to think this Deccan settlement one of the bright pages in the history of our Indian administration. The old plan was, we believe, substantially this :—the Government demand was pitched so high, that even in the most favourable seasons a large portion of it always remained unrealized. The cultivator, with an assessment hanging over him which he never could hope to pay, was of course entirely in the hands of the revenue officers. These latter, at the proper seasons, surveyed his crops, and, from the judgment they formed of them, assessed him for the year. Even this assessment was usually higher than it was found possible to collect, so that large remissions had frequently to be made, and considerable balances were left unrecovered.

The faults of such a system as this scarcely need to be pointed out. The constant meddling on the part of Government officials—the large number of these which the system rendered it necessary to employ—the slavish dependance in which the ryot was retained—the corruption and petty tyranny on the one hand, and the absence of manly and independent feeling, and, therefore, of energetic and enterprising industry on the other, were all necessary results of such arrangements. But, in addition to these, the revenue actually taken appears to have been on an average (although the rates in themselves were so small that an English farmer would laugh to hear them announced) decidedly greater than Marathi Kunbis, with such knowledge, skill, materials, means, and industrial habits as they possessed, were able to pay without slowly diminishing their means for future cultivation.

A well meant attempt at a better settlement, made many years ago, under the management of Mr. Pringle, failed altogether;—partly from the want of the requisite experience and skill in Mr. Pringle and his subordinates, and partly from the unprincipled character of the native agents employed—(the chief of whom, however, Mr. Pringle continued to patronise till the end of his career.)

We do not know very precisely the history of the present settlement. In the papers we have read on the subject the most prominent names appear to be those of Mr. Secretary Goldsmid, Captain Wingate, and Captain Davidson, and we are inclined—although, perhaps, without sufficient information to warrant us—to attribute the energy of purpose and persevering advocacy of the measure necessary to force it through some little opposition and a good deal of lukewarmness, to Mr. Goldsmid;—a great deal of the thinking, and most of the best writing on the subject, to Captain Wingate; and the invention of a variety of ingenious and excellent practical contrivances essential to the successful working of the measure, to Captain Davidson. If these gentlemen, however, do not agree with our estimate of their relative merits, we must request each of them to appropriate any portion of the praises we have awarded to his colleagues to which he may think himself entitled.

At the threshold of such an undertaking as a revenue settlement, the question which presents itself is, what is to be the nature of the revenue raised from the land? Is it to be a tax on raw produce, intended ultimately to fall on the consumer, a tax therefore on the necessaries of life—the most objectionable of all taxes? Or is it to be a (political economist's) rent, the least objectionable of any tax, and which, in a certain sense, may be said to fall upon nobody; but the economical effect of which is to maintain a remote approximation to equality among the cultivators, by taxing each man according to the advantages he starts with, and so, to prevent or retard the growth of a landed proprietary living merely on their rents?

The Indian Governments,—very much, no doubt, from the necessity of the case,—but, whether from that or from any other cause, with great propriety, as it seems to us, have decided, upon the latter—the least profitable lands in cultivation are taxed at a rate little more than nominal, (from three-pence to sixpence per acre,) and all others are supposed to pay the assessment on them from the surplus profit, which, from superior fertility, proximity to markets, convenience of carriage, &c., they would otherwise yield to the labour and capital of the cultivator.

Many of our native friends, and some of our European ones also, seem to us to labour under a strange confusion of ideas on this subject. They perceive that a remission of the Government land revenue would raise the holders of the best lands, the lands which pay the highest rates, to the rank of well-to-do landed proprietors;—that it might even enable the more fortunate of them to live, if they chose, in idleness, supported by the rent which their less fortunate brethren would then be willing to pay to obtain the superiority of fertility, situation, &c., of these better holdings. But they do not perceive that this could only be done by taxing themselves and the rest of the community to the full amount of all which these new landed proprietors would thus be enabled to appropriate ;—that their scheme is, at bottom, merely a proposition to levy taxes on the community generally, for no governmental purpose, either local or general, but to present in pure gift to a portion of the Kunbi population, in order to make independent gentlemen of them.

We advise those who make this proposal to study the iniquities to which this alienation—(or, as it was originally in that case, fraudulent appropriation)—of the lands of the country have given rise in England. A nobleman (an English Sirdar, Jaghirdar, or Enamdar) owns a few fields situated within a mile or two of one of the numerous centres of English trade and industry. He is originally bound in return for this property to render a variety of important services to the state. These services he contrives ultimately to shift entirely from himself to the general community, and taxes have to be raised to pay for their performance. In the meantime the skill, energy, and capital of the nation largely increase, and, with them, the population. Our nobleman's family contribute nothing to the national resources; they neither invent nor make the steam engines, the spinning jennies, the power looms, the railroads, nor any of the thousands of ingenious instruments and ingenious processes by which the wealth of the nation is created—they do not even achieve its wonderful conquests; but leave these latter to be obtained by a company of traders, one of whose original stipulations is, that they shall not be compelled to receive "Gentlemen" into their society, but shall be permitted to consort only with those of their own quality. Nevertheless, with the progress of the nation, the population of the trading and manufacturing town near our Jaghirdar's estate has at length extended itself so widely that the fields are required for houses, shops, and manufactories. These our Jaghirdar does not even build for the community. He finds a capitalist who undertakes to lease his ground for sixty years—to build on it such houses as the Jaghirdar stipulates for—to pay rent for the ground during the whole term, and at the end of it, to put the buildings into thorough repair, and make a perfectly gratuitous transfer of them to the Jaghirdar's family, who have contributed no iota towards the wealth of the country which has brought both these houses, and the population which inhabits them, and the revenues which pay for them, into existence;—and whose surveyor, before he releases the builder and temporary owner of the houses from his engagement, goes over them to see that they are left properly tiled, glazed, painted, and in every way in sound repair.

In this manner, while the whole revenue raised in British India, rent and taxes together, amounts to about twenty-three millions sterling, Great Britain, which might all be stowed away in the desert tract between the N. W. Provinces and the Indus, pays, first, fifty millions of rent to its Jaghirdars—and then, another fifty millions of taxes to its Government.

The evil now, too, is irremediable; for although the original possession of such a monopoly may in almost every instance be traced to either force or fraud, or a combination of both, the present owners have, in innumerable cases, the fair title of a free and full purchase of the property to plead. They, or their ancestors, have bought *what never ought to have been sold,* but which, being put up for sale, they of course must not be blamed for buying—viz.: the right and power, as the wealth of the nation increases, to sweep always a very large portion of this increase into their own coffers, and that without having necessarily contributed in the slightest degree towards its production.

Of the pleas which are usually urged in defence of such a social enormity as this, there is but one that has ever appeared to us to be worthy of any serious rejoinder. We look with great scorn and contempt on the pretence that a landed aristocracy is essential as an element in a free government, or to serve as models in all that concerns taste and manners. What can any community require in these respects which the *professional* aristocracy of Edinburgh—or such a *commercial* one as that of Liverpool—will not supply? But it is alleged that absolute property in the land is essential to secure the complete development of its resources. To this an obvious answer is, that, in England, the resources of the land are now, and have been, brought out by capitalist farmers, *who are not owners of the land they cultivate,* and who, in many cases, are (of course very absurdly) not even allowed a lease of it. If it be replied that although a landed aristocracy may successfully deal with such tenants, a nation or a government could not,—we answer, that with the superior intelligence and business habits of the present day, we do not see why it should not,—that although the difficulties of the task may be great, we believe that our revenue administrators, both here and in the N. W. Provinces, are at length successfully grappling with them; and that at all events we think it an experiment which should be very fully and fairly tried.

In considering a revenue system which professes to aim at absorbing the greater part of the *nett rent* of the country, whatever that may happen to amount to, one question which very naturally occurs is—if this rent yields a revenue greater than the necessities of the state require, how is the surplus to be appropriated? Unfortunately, this is not a question which will be of any practical importance in India for many a long day to come; we certainly hope to see the land revenue gradually increase, but while we have yet to find a substitute for the heavy and most objectionable tax on salt; to make thousands of miles of additional roads; to construct works that shall intercept, for the uses of the cultivator, and, in some cases, for internal navigation, the waters which now roll idly on both sides of India to the sea; to pay off the debt, and so force the capital now investedin it to seek productive employment, and thereby add to the resources of the country; and to provide funds for municipal purposes, and for the extension of the elements of a useful education to the great mass of the people; we can hardly anticipate, with the addition even of greatly increased economy in the Government expenditure, that, for many long years to come, the question of the disposal of a surplus revenue from rent can become a very urgent one. With our best wishes, however, that the day may soon arrive, we will now return to our surveyors and assessors.

The principal operations in the Deccan Survey and Assessment appear to be the following :—

I. The surface survey ; to determine, and mark permanently, the boundaries of each village and of each field.

II. A survey and estimate of the quality of the soil in each field ; and the assignment of a technical value to it per acre in an artificial scale of relative values ranging from an anna and a half to sixteen annas.

III. The division of the districts into groups of villages, such that those of each group may be supposed to possess nearly equal advantages of climate, markets, and convenience of carriage.

IV. The imposition on each group of villages of a total assessment, such as, from the past history of the group, it may fairly be expected to pay, and yet leave a considerable margin for the increase of the peasant's stock, and the consequent extension of cultivation.

V. A merely arithmetical operation—to wit, the assignment to each field of its share of the assessment in proportion to its size and its place in the scale of relative values.

The measurement of the cultivator's fields and the rates being thus determined, his *tenure* may be described as a lease, in which the landlord (the Government) binds itself for thirty years, neither to remove the tenant (provided that he pays his assessment,) nor to raise the assessment ; while it does not, on the other hand, bind the tenant, who is at liberty, at the commencement of each agricultural year, to throw up the whole or any portions of his holding, not less than a single field, and of course to take up any fields in the district which may be without a tenant.

Had the proposal for an extensive survey on this plan been originally laid before us, we should have ventured to pronounce, that with such agents as must necessarily be employed in this country, the operations described in our paragraph II. would be found impracticable,—that no system of checks that could be devised would insure sufficient attention to accuracy, sufficient uniformity of judgment, and sufficient freedom from corruption, to make the determinations under it of any practical value. There is pretty ample evidence, however, in the reports before us that these difficulties have been successfully met—and next to the general plan of the settlement, we consider the perseverance and skill displayed in working out this portion of it, to be the most meritorious feature connected with it.

Assuming the survey to have been completed according to the intentions of those who have planned and superintended it, the *tenure* would seem to present as favourable conditions for the development of an industrial spirit for the gradual accumulation of agricultural capital, and for improvements in the cultivation of the country, as any thing short of the introduction (of course an impossibility in this case) of intelligent capitalist farmers, and an altogether new race of cultivators could do. Any amount of agricultural progress may be obtained in England or Scotland on leases of twenty-one years, and leases which bind the farmer equally with his landlord. Of course no permanency or freedom of tenure can compensate for a really excessive assessment, and the security which exists against this in capitalist farming, from the necessity the landlord is under, in order to draw capital to his land, of offering terms which will allow of ordinary profits being realized, does not exist between a government and a race of mere peasant cultivators. Against this evil there is only the enlightened moderation, or enlightened selfishness, whichever you like, of the government to depend on. And the right amount of enlightenment we fancy has been very slow in coming. It seems, however, from the general tone of these papers to have arrived at last. No point is so frequently, or so earnestly urged in these reports as the pressing necessity which existed for large reductions in the rate of assessment, and the prudence even, to put the matter on no higher ground, of so lightly assessing the cultivator as to allow and induce him to increase his capital and extend his cultivation,—nor do we observe in any instance that the government has come to any other conclusion on this subject than the one recommended to them by the assessors.

In our next article we propose to allow the surveyors and assessors to speak for themselves.

No. II.

EXTRACTS FROM THE CHANDORE REPORT, FROM THE JOINT REPORT, AND FROM CAPTAIN WINGATE'S RECENT REPORT ON KHANDEISH.

FORMER REVENUE ARRANGEMENTS.

" 23. Three or four years after our acquisition of the country a new rental for each village was fixed, and the particular rates to be imposed to meet this new rental were determined. But, from all I can learn, it would appear that this settlement, although sanctioned by the European Officer in charge of these districts, was made by his Sheristedars, on the very imperfect information to be collected, in those early days of our rule, from the Hereditary Officers, and that neither a single village nor a single field was visited by the settling Officer or his native subordinates.

" 24. Although the rates to be imposed to meet this new rental were specified, there was no particularization of the divisions of lands on which these rates were to be imposed, and consequently, the responsible and delicate duty of determining, and that, too, annually, what fields should pay particular rates, was delegated to the Village Officers.

" 25. For instance, take a village supposed to contain, after deducting Mauphee, nine hundred Beeghas; of these one hundred are irrigated, and eight hundred dry land. The rental of this village was fixed by the settling Officer at, say, Rs. 1,115, and this sum was apportioned as follows :—

IRRIGATED LAND.

70 Beeghas at Rs. 5 per Beegha............	Rs. 350
30 Beeghas at Rs. 3 per Beegha............	„ 90
	Rs. 440

Dry Land.

400 Beeghas at Rs. 1 per Beegha............Rs. 400
300 Beeghas at Rs. ¾ per Beegha............ „ 225
100 Beeghas at Rs. ½ per Beegha............ „ 50

Rs. 675

Total Rental..............................Rs. 1,115
Total Beeghas of land subject to Assessment........ 900.

"The extent of dry land under cultivation might amount, in any one year to, say, four hundred Beeghas: it would remain for the Village Officers to determine as to the rates to be imposed thereon. Possibly they might enter, in their returns, that the whole of the one rupee land was lying waste, and assess these four hundred cultivated Beeghas at three-quarters, and half a rupee; or possibly they might assess half the cultivated land at one rupee, and half at three-quarters, and so on. The very same field which was taxed one year at half a rupee might the next season be assessed at the rate of one rupee.

"26. This new mode of management existed more on paper than in reality. The district and village authorities amusing the Collector with statements, exhibiting the apportionment of the revenue on the various fields according to these rates, while the villagers continued to adhere to their old and well-known payment by fractional shares."—*Mr. Goldsmid's Report in the Introductory Assessment of two Turufs in Chandore.*

THE NEW RATES.

"90. The rates on which I have determined for the two Turufs are, for

		First Class. R.	A.	P.	Lowest Class. R.	A.	P.	
Irrigated lands.	Patastul Bagaeet (XII. Classes.) per acre......	8	0	0	3	0	0	To cover the Government assessment and the cost Hucks of Hereditary Officers.
	Motustul Do. (V. Classes)	4	0	0	2	0	0	
Unirri-gated.	Jeeraeet (IX. Do.)......	1	8	0	0	2	3	

Ibid.

COMPARISON WITH PREVIOUS ASSESSMENT.

" 92. On referring to the diagram, it will be observed that the kumal or maximum amount of assessment realizable from the Government lands of the two Turufs is reduced fifty-two (52) per cent.; such reduction will no doubt appear enormous to those who do not understand that the former kumal never *was* realized, nor *never could* have been realized, and that any attempt to realize it would inevitably have brought ruin on the District.

" 93. The new rates will certainly effect a great reduction in the land assessment of the two Turufs, but such reduction the state of the District requires. I could write paragraph after paragraph, defending the imposition of a *moderate assessment*, but my doing so would be superfluous, as the sentiments I entertain on this subject are perfectly in unison with those of Government."—*Ibid.*

CLASSIFICATION OF FIELDS.

"14. Our classification requires not only a good eye and judgment to distinguish between the different gradations of soil, but also tact in estimating the proportions of each, in the field under inspection; and to the difficulty of this latter operation may be referred most of the errors brought to light by our system of check. We find, however, that such accuracy has been attained, as to reduce the errors arising from all sources so much, that the total error in a whole field rarely amounts to the difference between the value of two contiguous classes; and as we have nine of these, it is evident that such an error is inconsiderable, and cannot possibly vitiate the work; and the object of classification being to ascertain the relative values of different portions of land, this will be sufficiently attained, for practical purposes, when the resulting assessment is found not to interfere with cultivation, and where the waste lands of a district are uniformly brought under tillage, without any greater anxiety to obtain or shun particular fields being observable, than can be accounted for on considerations independent of the assessment.* And that this is the case here, we can abundantly prove; for in every district, and not in every district merely, but in every village, whatever its peculiarities of soil or situation, having any considerable portion of arable waste at the time of settlement, a marked extension of cultivation has subsequently taken place."—*Joint Report.*

"16. In the North Western Provinces further modifications have been made in the assessment of particular estates, in order to accommodate the present settlement to that previously existing, and which appear to have been rendered necessary by the marked difference of industry and agricultural skill in the various communities of proprietors and cultivators located in the different villages.

Vide 92 para of Suddur Board's Revenue circular, dated 9th April 1839.

"The Board regret the existence of such a necessity, and it has been their object to equalize, as far as possible, the Government demand. Here, however, such marked distinctions in the several classes of cultivators are not observable, and have never been recognized as a reason for exemption from assessment. The modifications in question are therefore happily unnecessary, and all villages possessing equal advantages of position, water, soil, and climate, have been assessed alike."

THE ASSESSMENT IS NOT THE WHOLE OF THE RENT.

"17. From the difficulty of ascertaining the true rent of different descriptions of land, we have not assumed any theoretical proportion of this for the standard of our assessment; but we fully coincide in the justice of the principle of limiting the Government demand to a portion of the true rent, and believe 50 to 80 per cent. thereof, as laid down by the Board, would form a liberal assessment, and that this principle, if capable of being

* In choosing a field, a ryot does not look to the assessment alone, but also to the convenience of its position with reference to the rest of the farm, and many other evident considerations, which it is needless to particularize.

carried into practice, would prove an invaluable blessing to the agricultural classes of India, and introduce a new era in their history. And we further ascribe to the fact of a portion of the rent having been seldom, if ever, left to the proprietor or cultivator in India, the characteristic wretchedness of its agricultural population, rather than to any peculiarities marking its different systems of revenue management."—*Ibid.*

ADVANTAGES OF THE FIELD ASSESSMENT OVER THE VILLAGE SYSTEM.

"6. The superior advantages of the field assessment over that by which the assessment is placed on the whole lands of a village, or the entire holdings of individuals or co-partners, whether proprietors or occupants, have been already so fully stated by two of our number, in their joint report, and are so generally admitted by the Revenue Officers of this presidency, that we deem it unnecessary to enter upon any very detailed exposition of them here. It may be permitted us to remark, however, that one manifest advantage of breaking up the assessment of a village into portions so minute, is the facility it affords to the cultivators of contracting or enlarging their farms from year to year, according to the fluctuating amount of agricultural capital and stock at their disposal; which is of incalculable importance to farmers possessed of so limited resources as those of the cultivating classes throughout India.

"7. The loss of a few bullocks by disease, or other causes, may quite incapacitate a ryot from cultivating profitably the extent of land he had previously in tillage, and without the privilege of contracting the extent of his farm, and consequent liabilities on occasion of such losses, his ruin would be very shortly consummated. It is for this reason that there would be no advantage, but the contrary, in binding down the cultivators by long leases, as has often been recommended. The only advantage of a long lease to a farmer, is the security it affords against any increase of rent or assessment during its continuance; while on the other hand, it has the disadvantage of increasing his risk and liabilities, in proportion to the length of the period for which it makes him responsible for the rent or assessment. The longer the lease, the greater the scope for the employment of capital, but the greater the liabilities of the farmer, and risk of failure. With farmers of large capital, the security of tenure will over-balance the risk: but with farmers of small capital the case will be reversed; and for the latter class of men in any country it may safely be predicted that long leases, binding them to pay an invariable rent for a long series of years, are quite unsuitable.

"8. To all classes of farmers, however, whether rich or poor, the tenure which affords the greatest security against increase of rent, with the least extent of liability and risk of loss, is undoubtedly that most favourable to the interest of the agricultural classes, and to the progressive increase of farming capital; and it is evident that this can only be effected by shifting the risk from the tenant to the landlord, and securing to the former all the advantages and security of a long lease, without its attendant liabilities. In countries where the land is divided into properties of limited extent, landlords could not be expected to incur this risk, when it is so easy to shift it on their tenants and secure their own rents; but the case is altogether different when the whole, or a large portion, of the land rent is levied by Government. In the latter case, the interests of the rent-payer and rent-receiver are identical; with a Government, the question is not the certainty and amount of rent derivable from one estate, without reference to aught beyond its boundaries, but from the country at large. The land-tax is obtained, not from a few individual farmers, but from the whole agricultural community: and its amount will fluctuate with the circumstances of the latter. With every diminution of the total amount of capatal employed in agriculture, the land revenue will decline: with every increase, it will improve. The maximum of farming capital and land revenue will be the same, as will also be their fluctuations. It appears, therefore, that in opposition to the case of an ordinary landowner, Government incurs neither risk of loss, nor additional liabilities, by giving the cultivator all the advantages of a long lease, and at the same time relieving him of its attendant disadvantages.

"9. The important end here pointed out, we believe to be fully attained by the fixed field assessment of our surveys, administered by annual leases. The cultivator's title to the occupation of his fields is indestructible, while he continues to discharge the assessment laid upon them, though his engagement for each be annually renewed; and by placing the assessment upon each field, instead of on his whole holding, he his enabled, when circumstances make the course desirable, to relinquish any of the former, or take up others which may be unoccupied, so as to accommodate the extent of his liabilities to his means to meet them. The fixed field assessment for the term of thirty years, introduced by our surveys, thus secures to the cultivator the full advantages of a thirty years' lease, without burdening him with any condition beyond that of discharging the assessment for the single year to which his engagement extends. He has thus all the security of tenure which the longest lease could confer, without the attendant liabilities and risk, which his limited capital and precarious circumstances would be quite inadequate to meet."—*Ibid.*

PRINCIPLES WHICH GUIDE THE ASSESSOR IN FIXING THE RATES.

"66. We have now defined, with as great a degree of minuteness as we consider desirable, the various operations of the survey, undertaken for the purpose of distributing the assessment over the fields into which the lands of each village are divided, with reference to their extent and capabilities; it now remains for us to point out what we deem the best mode of fixing the absolute amount of assessment to be so distributed. The first question for consideration is, the extent of territory for which a uniform standard of assessment should be fixed. This will depend upon the influences we admit into consideration with a view to determine the point. Among the most important of these influences may be ranked climate, position with respect to markets, agricultural skill, and the actual condition of the cultivators. The first of these may be considered permanent; the second and the third less so; and the fourth, in a great measure, temporary; and as our settlements are intended to be of considerable duration, there is an obvious advantage in regulating the assessment by considerations of a permanent character, or, at least, such as are not likely to undergo any very material change during the term of years, generally 30, for which it is to endure.

"67. In determining, then, upon the extent of country to be assessed at uniform rates, we are of opinion that the more permanent distinctions of climate, markets, and husbandry, should receive our chief attention. We should not think of imposing different rates of assessment on a tract of country similarly situated in respect to these three points, in consequence of the actual condition of the cultivators varying in different parts of it. Were we to do so, we should depart from the principle, laid down by the Hon'ble Court of Directors, of assessing land according to its capabilities, and adopt the objectionable one of doing so with reference to the means of the person holding it. The effect of such a system, by creating different rates of profit upon capital employed in agriculture, would interfere with its natural and most advantageous distribution, by diverting it from lands, actually in cultivation, to the lowly-assessed waste of those villages of which the cultivators happen to be poor. By enabling the latter to meet the Government demands, without the application of the same degree of capital and skill required in the case of better cultivated villages, it would foster in the former a slovenly and unremunerative mode of husbandry. By taking into account an element so uncertain and liable to change as the condition of the cultivators in particular villages, the assessment would become less and less suitable, with every improvement in their condition. On the other hand, by basing the assessment on considerations of a durable character, we have the promise of its remaining suitable for a lengthened period, and at the expiration of the term for which it is confirmed, requiring no further alteration than a simple increase or decrease of its amount, as the exigencies of the country and Government might demand.

"68. Each Collectorate being divided into districts, of which the management and records are distinct, it is an obvious advantage to consider the assessment of each of these divisions separately; and were the points bearing on the distribution of the Government demand alike in all parts of any such division, one standard of assessment would be suitable for the whole.

But this is seldom the case : and there is usually such marked distinction between different portions of the same district as to require the assessment to be regulated with reference to these. The first question, then, in proceeding to the assessment of a district, is to ascertain whether such distinctions exist, and to define the limits over which they prevail. This, however, will seldom be a task of much difficulty, or involving any very minute investigations, as marked differences only, calling for an alteration in the rates of assessment, require notice : and within the limits of a single district three to four classes of villages would generally be found ample for this purpose.

"69. The relative values of the fields of each village having been determined from the classification of soils, the command of water for irrigation, or other extrinsic circumstances, and the villages of a district arranged into groups, according to their respective advantages of climate, markets, &c., it only remains, in order to complete the settlement, to fix the absolute amount of assessment to be levied from the whole.

"70. The determination of this point is, perhaps, the most important and difficult operation connected with the survey, and requires, beyond all others, the exercise of great judgment and discrimination on the part of the Officer on whom it devolves. The first requisite is to obtain a clear understanding of the nature and effects of our past management of the district, which will be best arrived at by an examination and comparison of the annual revenue settlements of as many previous years as trustworthy data may be procurable for, and from local inquiries of the people, during the progress of the survey. The information collected on the subject of past revenue settlements should be so arranged as to enable us to trace with facility the mutual influence upon each other of the assessment, the collections, and the cultivation.

"This, in our opinion, can best be done by the aid of diagrams,* constructed so as to exhibit, in contiguous columns, by linear proportions, the amount and fluctuations of the assessment, collec-

* The information here alluded to by Captain Wingate as given "by the aid of a diagram," is given, farther on, in certain figured statements which follow.

tions, and cultivation, for each of the years to which they relate, so as to convey to the mind clear and definite conceptions of the subject, such as it is scarcely possible to obtain from figured statements, even after the most laborious and attentive study. The information to be embodied in the diagram best suited for our purpose should be restricted to the land of the district subject to the full assessment; the extent of this cultivated in each year; the assessment on the same, and the portion of the assessment actually realised. This will exclude from the diagram several items of revenue obtained from this land, such as the rent of grazing farms, fruit trees, sheep tax, &c., independent of the assessment hitherto levied on the cultivated land, which is the proper object of our present inquiry.

"72. The hucks of hereditary officers upon cultivated land, however, having to be included in the survey assessment, and as forming a real addition to the burdens on the land, might appropriately be included in the diagram; but as no authentic records of the amount of such hucks actually realised are obtainable, we think it preferable to omit them, and to estimate separately the addition to be made on their account to the collections shown by the diagram.

"73. The items of information admitted into the diagram should be alike for each year. They should have reference to the same villages; and in the event of any having lapsed to Government, or having been otherwise transferred during the period embraced in the diagram, for which information for all the years required cannot be obtained, such villages should be excluded altogether; or if it be considered preferable to include them, a proportionate increase should be made to the entries of the diagram in the case of the years for which exact data may be wanting. The cultivation and assessment for each year should be estimated in the same land measures, and the same currency, and an explanation of the value of these afforded. [Collections or remissions on account of outstanding balances, should be included in the entries of the year to which they relate, though made at a future period.] Every care should be taken to secure the accuracy of the information embodied in the diagram, and the points which may be considered imperfect brought to notice.

"74. Furthermore, to assist in tracing the causes to which the prosperity or decline of villages, or tracts containing several villages, are to be attributed, independent statements of the annual revenue settlements of each village should be prepared, and from these, again, a general statement for the whole district, or any portion of it, should be framed, and its accuracy tested by a comparison with the general accounts of the Talooka, and from the return, so prepared and corrected, the diagram should finally be constructed. The nature and amount of the various items of land revenue and hucks excluded from the diagram, should be separately noted, and taken into account in considering the financial results of the proposed assessment.

"75. And, finally, with the view of affording the fullest information on this important subject, detailed figured statements should be furnished, exhibiting the source and amount of every item of revenue hitherto derived from land of every description, whether Government or alienated, comprised within the limits of the villages for which an assessment is proposed.

"76. The information thus collected and exhibited, with that obtained by local inquiries into the past history of the district, will generally enable us to trace the causes which have affected its past condition; and a knowledge of these, aided by a comparison of the capabilities of the district with those of others in its neighbourhood, will lead to a satisfactory conclusion regarding the amount of assessment to be imposed.

"77. But, instead of a particular sum at which a district should be assessed, it amounts to the same thing, and is more convenient, to determine the rates to be imposed on the several descriptions of soil and culture contained within its limits, so as to produce the amount in question. And to do this, it is only requisite to fix the maximum rates for the different descriptions of cultivation, when, of course, inferior rates will be at once deducible from the relative values of our classification scales.

"78. The rates so determined should be applied to all descriptions of land, alienated as well as otherwise: for the settlement could not be considered complete, unless the extent and value of aliented land, as well as that under the immediate management of Government, were ascertained and recorded. When the calculation of the assessment from the rates is completed, field registers, embodying the results of the survey, should be prepared for each village separately, for the use of the collectors. These, and the village maps, form a complete record of our operations ; and while they and the field boundaries exist, all the important data resulting from the survey will be preserved."—*Ibid.*

REVENUE MANAGEMENT.

RULES.

" I.—With a view to the improvement of the country and people, the assessment now introduced by the Superintendent Revenue Survey, has been fixed by Government for a period of thirty years, viz., from Fuslee to during which period the full benefit of every improvement, such as the conversion of dry into irrigated land by the digging or repairing of wells and tanks, the planting of fruit-trees, &c., will be secured to the incumbent of the land, and no extra assessment levied on that account.

" II.—All cesses upon land have been absorbed in the new assessment ; consequently, when there are fruit-trees in a field, their produce is to be taken by the cultivator, and nothing beyond the assessment placed on the field levied on that account from him ; but in the case of valuable fruit and other trees standing in fields assessed at dry crop rates, and not in cultivation at the introduction of the survey, and the produce of which it has hitherto been customary to sell on account of Government, the right of property in these trees and of occupancy in the field, should be offered at a fair upset price, and sold once for all by public auction to the highest bidder, and nothing in excess of the survey assessment thereafter exacted. But, if no one offer to undertake the cultivation of the field on these terms, the produce of the trees may be sold annually, according to custom.

" III.—No field is to be let for less than the full survey assessment, on account of its having been long waste, overrun with jungle, or any other reason whatever.

"IV.—In the survey registers, in the case of fields containing garden and rice land, the said land is entered at so many acres bearing a certain assessment, or the latter is laid upon the well in the case of garden land, without the irrigated acres being specified. This assessment is invariably to be levied, and nothing more, whether a greater or less number of acres, or none at all, be cultivated with garden or rice crops; and should there, now or hereafter, be garden or rice land in any field not entered as having such in the survey registers, no extra assessment is to be levied on that account, the dry crop assessment therein entered is alone to be levied. In the registers, also, a deduction is made on account of barren land in certain fields, and the assessment placed on the arable land alone; but, in event of the cultivator bringing any portion of the land deducted as barren into cultivation, no extra assessment is to be levied on that account; the assessment on the field entered in the register is alone to be levied.

"V.—Every cultivator in whose name any field, or share of a field, on whatever tenure held, is entered in the village cultivation returns, is to be considered the holder of such field or share; and so long as he shall continue to pay the survey assessment due on it, he cannot be ejected or deprived of his right by any revenue authority; but, in event of his failing to discharge the full assessment, Government reserves the power of ejecting him from any field or share of which the assessment shall at least be equal to the balance outstanding, the defaulter retaining, however, the privilege of determining the particular field or fields to be so relinquished; and in cases when the tenure precludes summary ejectment, the collector will observe the forms necessary to give his orders the force of a legal decree.

"VI.—In event of a holder of Government land dying, his fields or shares are to be entered in the name of his eldest son or next heir, should he or his representatives agree to take them.

"VII.—When two ryots hold a field, and one of them relinquishes his share, or dies without heirs, the share thus lapsing is to be offered, in the first instance, to the other sharer before it is offered to any other party; and, in event of the said sharer declining it, and no other party applying to take it up, the former must relinquish his share too, and allow the whole field to become waste.

"VIII.—When there are more sharers than two in a field, and any of them relinquishes a share, or dies without heirs, it should be offered, as above, to the sharers in the first instance, beginning, in event of their failing to settle the matter amongst themselves, with the largest sharer, and so on to the least. If none of these, nor any other party, be found to take up the relinquished share, the whole field must be thrown up.

"IX.—Whoever has a field or portion of one entered in his name in the Government accounts, may have the said field or portion transferred to the name of any other person agreeing to cultivate the same, on his making a written application to that effect in the usual 'razeenama,' or petition to resign.

"X.—Proprietors of Enam, Joodee, and Meeras lands, having possession of the same, have the right of cutting down or otherwise disposing of all trees growing therein, and also holders of Government fields, of which they have been in uninterrupted occupancy from a period anterior to the age of the trees, or for a period of 20 years, or who have purchased the trees under the provisions of Rule 2.

"XI.—Holders of Government fields besides those specified in the preceding rule, or occupants of Meeras, Joodee, or Enam lands, holding the same from Government, must obtain permission to cut down trees, and will, in event of permission being given, be required to plant two trees for every one cut, unless exempted from this condition by order of the Collector. The permission to cut trees under this rule, and also trees in Government waste fields, for any purpose connected with agricultural operations, to be granted by the Patel and Koolcurnee on application, a record thereof being kept for the inspection of Government officers. For other actual and immediate wants of the villagers, such as repair of houses, &c., permission to be obtained from the Mamlutdar or Mahálkuree; but for cutting any large number, or for any purpose of sale or profit, the permission of the Collector or one of his assistants to be necessary, when any conditions which may appear advisable can be imposed.

"XII.—In taking up waste for cultivation, a ryot must agree for a whole survey field at the full assessment, and no portion of a field is, on any account, to be given for this purpose, except in the case mentioned in the next rule; and when two or more cultivators agree together to cultivate a waste field, it must be entered in the name of one of their number, who will be considered the holder, unless the assessment of the field amount to, or exceed, 20 Rupees, in which case it may be entered in the names of two or more holders, on the condition that the assessment of the share of each shall in no case fall short of 10 Rupees.

"XIII.—There are some survey fields, consisting in great part of land covered with dense jungle, or otherwise unsuited in their present state for cultivation, upon which no assessment is placed on the survey registers. In the event of portions of such fields being brought under cultivation, rates of Assessment should be fixed by the Mamlutdar upon the acres under tillage, equivalent to those of similar soils in the same village. This rule applies to all fields in the survey registers on which rates of assessment have not been fixed.

"XIV.—Unless special exceptions be made by the Collector, of valuable grass lands, certain to realize rents in excess of the survey assessment, the grazing of all waste of Government and Meeras land is annually to be sold by auction, field by field, at the commencement of the monsoon, a preference being given, at the sale, to the inhabitants of the village to which the lands may belong. The bidding, however, for any waste field should not be allowed to go beyond its assessment in the survey register, and when it reaches this point, the field should be entered in the name of the last bidder, as other cultivated land held at the full Assessment, and the person so taking it a dmitted to all the privileges of a holder of land under tillage.

"XV.—The grass of fields especially excepted by the Collector from the operation of the preceding rule, may be sold by auction to any one, for sums in excess of the survey assessment.

"XVI.—The grazing of the unarable and other fields not subjected to Assessment in the survey register, should be sold by auction by the Collector as in the preceding rule, a reasonable proportion being set aside for the free pasturage of such villages as have hitherto enjoyed this right.

"XVII.—In some villages houses are attached to particular fields, and it has been customary to oblige a ryot, throwing up one of these fields, to relinquish his house at the same time. This custom, however, is now abolished; and every cultivator is at liberty to throw up any field without his title to his house being at all affected thereby. This rule does not apply to the case of alienated lands.

"XVIII.—In the survey register an assessment is placed on Joodee and Enam, as well as Government fields, but the Joodeedars and Enamdars are not bound thereby, and are at liberty to let out their lands on any terms they please.

"XIX.—In event of Enam land being confiscated, or temporarily attached, it is to be let out, while under Government management, at the survey assessment, or sold by auction, if waste, exactly as Government land. This rule does not apply to the year in which the attachment is effected, for which the existing agreements made with the Enamdar should be allowed to stand.

"XX.—Cultivators wishing to relinquish fields must give in written applications to that effect before the first of May, and with the view of ensuring this being done, the village Officers are to assemble all the holders of Government land on the 30th of April n each year, and having explained to them that it is the last day on which resignations will be received, the Koolkurnee shall then and there write out, in a prescribed form, which must specify the number, acres, and assessment of every field to be relinquished, the 'Razeenama' (or petitions to resign,) for any parties requiring them. These petitions should be signed or authenticated in the presence of one or more witnesses, by the parties making them, and countersigned by the Patel and Koolkurnee, who should forward them without delay to the Mamlutdar, or Mahalkurree, by whom they are to be attested and returned to the Village Officers, as vouchers for any alteration made in the village accounts of the following year. When waste fields are wanted for cultivation, written applications must, in like manner, be taken from the applicants, countersigned by the Village Officers, and forwarded by them to the Mamlutdar or Mahalkurree, by whom they are to be attested and returned, and all these resignations of cultivated, and applications for waste fields, are to be produced at each Jumabundee settlement, for examination. But Village Officers, under pain of punishment, are not to make any alterations in the cultivation registers, except upon the authority of the vouchers mentioned above, or in obedience to written instructions from the Mamlutdar or Mahalkurree.

"XXI. The revenue should be collected by fixed instalments, without reference to the proportion of early or late crops grown in any one year; and, consequently, no field inspection for the purpose of obtaining such information should be made. In districts where early crops prevail, we recommend the collections to be made in four equal instalments, falling due on 15th December, 1st February, 15th March, and 1st May; and, where early and late crops are nearly equal, or the latter predominate, we also recommend four equal instalments, but respectively falling due a month later, viz: on 15th January, 1st March, 15th April, and 1st June.

"XXII. The field boundary marks erected at the survey should be preserved with the greatest care, and when injured, timely repairs must be made by the cultivators in the case of cultivated lands, and by hired labourers in the case of waste, the expense of the latter being defrayed from a sum of 100 Rs., to be deducted for the purpose from the proceeds of the grazing farms of each Talooka, as sanctioned by Government. This amount should therefore be placed in deposit each year, and the order of the Collector obtained for its expenditure, as above explained, wherever necessary. The intervening strips connecting the boundary marks of a breadth corresponding with the latter, are constituted the boundary of the field, and forbidden to be ploughed over or otherwise injured; and in the case of dry crop lands, before preparing any field for sowing, these strips are to be distinctly marked off each year, by the holder running his plough along the boundary. In the event of this order being neglected, and this space ploughed up or sown, the cultivator is to be made to connect the two contiguous marks, between which the boundary had been disregarded, by a continuous ridge of earth, 1½ foot in height; and should he fail to do so within a certain number of days, the Village Officers are to report the circumstance to the Mamlutdar, who is to apply to the Collector for a notice to be served on the holder of the field, according to the provisions of Act III. of 1846; and if this be disregarded, the boundary is to be put up by hired labourers, and the amount recovered from him, as therein provided."

No. III.

REPLY BY CAPTAIN WINGATE TO CERTAIN OBJECTIONS.

Appendix to Joint Report.

"5. You will observe, by referring to Rule 5 of the Joint Report, that the only way in which the title of a cultivator to any field can be vitiated, is through his failing to discharge the assessment laid upon it. And he will be called upon to pay this assessment upon every field entered in his name in the village books, without reference at all to the circumstance of its being waste or cultivated. So long as he pays the assessment, no field can, under any circumstances, be struck or left out of his holding, except upon his own written application to that effect, under the provisions of Rule 20; and it will thus be evident that no rival or other party could by possibility step in and supplant him in the way supposed by Government. It seems to me difficult to imagine a more secure title to occupancy than this. It is absolutely free from all conditions, except the simple one of discharging the Government land tax, and this condition, it is evident, could not be dispensed with under any plan of management whatever.

"6. The occupant is moreover wholly relieved from the interference or surveillance of the Government Officers. Their power is limited to the collection of the assessment due from him for the land entered in his name. They cannot demand more or less, nor even the assessment itself, except at the stated periods fixed for the collections. So long as he is ready with the money due at such times, they have absolutely no power at all of meddling in his affairs. They have no right to interrogate him as to whether his fields are waste or cultivated, his crops good or bad. The payment of his assessment affords a valid and sufficient answer to all objectors. A more completely independent position for a farmer to occupy than this it is hard to imagine. His own industry provides the means of paying his assessment, and he is absolutely free to exert this industry as may seem to him best, without having occasion to defer to the wishes or ideas of any one. I believe that in no country of the world are the cultivators so thoroughly independent as they will be in our surveyed districts, when the rules of the Joint Report shall be fully enforced. In the Dharwar Collectorate, where they are already in operation for the most part, their effect is readily observable in the bold bearing the cultivators quickly assume toward their village officers, and other influential parties, subsequent to the introduction of the new settlement.

"27. Government think it preferable the periods to be fixed for the payment of the instalments forming the subject of Rule 21 be disposed of apart from the ordinary Survey Rules; and though not disposed to dissent from this arrangement, I would yet respectfully submit that the settlement of those periods is of very great importance to the success of the survey settlements, and I trust, therefore, it will not be considered irrelevant to offer in this place the following arguments in favor of those fixed by Rule 21. The proposed instalments would fall due on the 15th December, 1st February, 15th March, and 1st May, in the case of districts when the early crops on an average of season predominate, and a month later, viz., on 15th January, 1st March, 15th April, and 1st June in the remaining districts. Three principal objects were in view in selecting the periods in question: Firstly, to enable the cultivator to provide funds for the payment of his assessment from *bona fide* sales of produce; Secondly, to distribute the collections over a period of six months, instead of four, as at present is generally the case, in order to afford the cultivator greater facilities for the disposal of his produce, and prevent prices becoming needlessly lowered during the collecting season, by forcing sales of produce at a sacrifice, which will always be the case when the instalments follow each other too closely; Thirdly, to have the instalments invariable, under all circumstances, for each district, that the cultivators may be taught to use foresight, and adopt timely measures for providing the funds necessary to the liquidation of their rents, by removing the uncertainty, and opportunities for jobbing and favoritism, attendant on the plan of collecting the revenue by variable instalments, according to the report of village officers as to the proportion of early and late crops grown in each particular season. All of these objects I deem very important; and all will, it seems to me, be fully attained without the entailment of any countervailing disadvantages, by the adoption of the periods for the collection of the instalments mentioned in the Rule.

"28. In the earliest districts, viz., those lying immediately East of the Ghauts, in which the whole crop, with some few exceptions, belongs to the early harvest, no part of it could be got ready for market and sold much before the 15th of December; but, by making an effort, a cultivator could manage to sell by that time sufficient produce to make up the 1st instalment, which is only one-fourth of his whole assessment. An earlier date, then, than the 15th of December, could not be fixed upon anywhere, without defeating one main object of the Rule, which is to enable the assessment to be provided by actual sales of produce, instead of by funds taken up at an excessive rate of interest from money lenders. In these early districts a considerable portion of the crop would be ready for market before the 1st February, and there would be no difficulty in selling it in time to provide the 2nd, 3rd, and 4th instalments. In the case of the later districts, there would be everywhere a sufficient proportion of early crops grown to furnish the means of paying the 1st instalment, falling due on 15th January, and the late crops could be got ready and sold in time for the payment of the remaining three instalments.

"29. In the case of both early and late crops, I feel assured that the adoption of a shorter interval than six weeks between each instalment would either have the effect of forcing sales of produce, and bringing down prices, or of driving the cultivators to the money-lenders, from the want of time and opportunity to dispose of a sufficient portion of their crop to meet each succeeding instalment. I have frequently conversed with intelligent cultivators on this subject, and they have always been sensible of the great advantage that would result to them from lengthening the intervals between the instalments from a month to six weeks, and have freely admitted that under such circumstances they would never have occasion to borrow, or dream of doing so, in order to raise money for the payment of their rents."

These extracts, we think, reflect the highest credit on the writers of the reports. We have seldom seen more masterly—and never more liberal and enlightened—specimens of state-craft; and we could wipe out a good many of our old grudges against Mr. Goldsmid in consideration of his appreciation and steady support of such views as these, and of whatever share he may have had in originating them.

We must also extract Captain Wingate's bird's-eye view of Khandeish, given at the commencement of his recent report. With the assistance of a flying trip which we once made into the province, and knowing something of the Deccan, with which Captain Wingate continually compares it, his sketch appears to realize it to us, both physically and socially, so vividly, that we could almost fancy ourselves old residents in it.

"The Collectorate of Khandeish contains sixteen Talooks, viz. Sowda, Yawal, Chopra, Thalneir, and Sooltanpoor, situated in the order I have named them from east to west, along the north bank of the Taptee River; Nusseerabad, Errundole, Amulneir, and Nundoorbar, occupying a similar position along the southern bank of the same river; and Jamneir, Burgaon, Chaleesgaon, Dhoolia, Malligaon, Pimpulneir, and Baglan, lying between the Taptee Talooks and the Chandore or Adjunta range of hills which divides Khandeish from the Deccan.

"The fall of rain throughout Khandeish is probably less than in the Southern Maharatta country, and little, if at all, greater than in the Deccan, while the rocks and the soils are exactly similar to those of the latter province, though the harder varieties of trap are much more sparingly distributed in Khandeish than in the Deccan. Notwithstanding, however, these resemblances, the soil of Khandeish is more fertile, and yields heavier crops than that of either the Deccan or the Southern Mahratta country, which, apparently, is owing to some unexplained peculiarity of climate, and to the soil being less exhausted by long-continued cultivation.

"This superior fertility, however, does not affect the relative fertility of the several varieties of soil amongst themselves. The principal crops of Khandeish are also those of the Deccan and Southern Mahratta country, and the modes of husbandry do not materially differ; on which account the plan for estimating the relative values of different kinds of soil followed in the surveys of those provinces will be, in all respects, applicable to Khandeish.

"Irrigation is more extensively practised in Khandeish than in the Deccan or Southern Mahratta country. The valleys of Khandeish are all open and level, and the smaller rivers, taking their rise in the Western Ghauts, flow in shallow beds, which are every here and there obstructed by ledges of hard rocks. These act as natural dams, and afford great facilities for the construction of bundharas, or masonry dams, for diverting the water of the river into canals for irrigation. Bundharas have, accordingly, been built in great numbers in these rivers, and more particularly in the Talooks of Baglan, Pimpulneir, Malligaon, and Dhoolia. A masonry wall of a few feet in height, built across the bed of the river at some place where there is a natural ledge of rocks, affords a sufficient head of water to admit of the stream being led off by a canal so as to rise above the level of the plain from two to three miles lower down. The flatness of the land, and its very gentle slope in the direction of the course of the river, adapts it admirably for irrigation, and in the case of all the bundharas I have seen there is much greater extent of land admitting of being overflowed than the supply of water suffices to irrigate. All the Khandeish rivers flow into the Taptee, but the bundharas are chiefly found on the upper portions of their courses. The river beds become gradually deeper as they approach the Taptee; and so, unfavourable for the construction of dams. The Taptee itself flows in a channel of extraordinary depth, depressed at least a hundred feet below the level of the plain through which it flows; and its waters are, therefore, not available for irrigation in any part of their passage through Khandeish.

" Water is obtainable by digging almost everywhere in Khandeish, and wells at one time have been very numerous. The Taptee, however, acts as a drain to carry off the subsoil waters, and the wells gradually deepen as they approach that river, until their water can no longer be profitably used for irrigation. Accordingly, in the immediate neighbourhood of the Taptee, wells are rarely met with, and, even at distances of 8 to 10 miles from the river, they are 50 and 60 feet in depth in the Chopra Talook. Generally speaking, however, their depth is much less considerable, and at some future day, when the wants of an increasing population shall exceed the capabilities of the land to supply without the aid of irrigation, water will be obtainable in unlimited quantity by the digging of wells. The " Mothusthul," or well irrigation, is even now considerable; but, excepting in the immediate neighbourhood of towns, where there is a demand for garden produce, I am inclined to think it the least remunerative husbandry in Khandeish.

" The irrigated husbandry is, however, of quite subordinate importance to that of the dry crop. ' Gool,' or coarse sugar, and opium, are the chief exports belonging to the former, whereas all the great exports of Khandeish,—cotton, oil-seeds, wheat, gram, and formerly indigo,—belong to the latter; though wheat and gram are also grown, to some extent, on irrigated land.

" The early, or monsoon crops, are by far the most important in Khandeish, and to them belong all the dry crop exports I have named, except wheat, gram, and linseed; formerly the late, or rubbee crops, used to be much more extensively grown than is now the case, but wheat and gram have been displaced to a great extent by cotton, owing to the comparatively large demand for the latter crop, of late years.

" The extent of cultivation in Khandeish, compared with its area, is very limited. On entering the province from almost any quarter, the face of the country appears to be covered with low scattered bush-jungle. This jungle is composed of various kinds of thorny bushes, of which the 'bear,' with its recurved thorns, is the most abundant. These bushes are seldom more than ten feet in height, and usually much less. They do not generally grow very close together, but here and there dense and almost impervious thickets are met with.

"On viewing the country around from any little elevation, it is difficult to make out where the cultivation is situated, as the sombre monotonous jungle meets the eye in every direction. This is accounted for by the fields being frequently surrounded by strips of waste covered with jungle, and by the cultivated fields themselves being often half covered with bear-thorn bushes. When a field is prepared for cultivation in Khandeish, the bushes covering the surface are not rooted out, but are merely cut down to the ground, and the plough is driven among the stumps, as in an American clearing. The vitality of the bush seems to be little affected by the operation, it begins to sprout again with the growing crop, and in six months' time seems almost as large and as vigorous as before it was cut down; and after the crop is cut, the field wears the look of being covered with jungle much as before. When the field is next prepared for sowing, the bushes are again cut down, and again spring up, and so the alternation goes on. In time, no doubt, the bushes would be destroyed by this constant pruning, but in consequence of the great abundance of arable land in Khandeish, the same land is not usually cropped for more than three or four years in succession. It is then thrown up, as the soil begins to yield a diminished return, and a piece of fresh waste is taken instead. The fields thus thrown up are allowed to lie fallow for several years before they are again taken into cultivation.

"This mode of husbandry does not eradicate the bush jungle, and in a year or two after a field so cultivated is relinquished the jungle has grown up as thickly as ever, and there is nothing to indicate that the field has ever been under tillage at all. It is only immediately around the villages, in thinly peopled parts, that the fields are in continuous cultivation, as there the facilities for manuring and bringing home the crops make such lands more valuable than those at a greater distance, even with the advantage of the greater productive capabilities of the soil occasioned by long fallows. Generally, then, throughout Khandeish, with an exception to be described presently, there is a limited space tolerably cleared around each inhabited village, and all the rest of the country, whether cultivated or waste, is more or less overrun with low bush-jungle, which would form a serious hinderance to detailed survey operations.

"The exception to which I have alluded is the upper part of the fine rich plain of the Taptee, which, for some miles on both sides of the river, in the Talooks of Sowda, Yawul, part of Chopra, Nusseerabad, Errundole, and part of Amulneir, is cleared of jungle, and for the most part under cultivation. This is the best peopled and richest portion of, and, I may say, the only part of, the Collectorate, that looks like an old country. All the rest has more the aspect of a newly-peopled colony, if we except the traces of a former industry to be seen in the mango and tamarind trees, and the many ruined wells which are still to be met with in the neighbourhood of almost every village.

"Excepting, then, the well-cultivated portion of the Taptee plain above referred to, the whole of Khandeish may be viewed as only very partially reclaimed from a state of nature. The present population is wholly inadequate to occupy it fully, and there is no prospect, I should say, of the population becoming sufficient for this purpose for the next century to come. To make this evident, it will be necessary to refer more particularly to the present population and cultivation of the several Talooks of the Collectorate.

"The data for the following Table have been obtained from returns furnished to me by the Collector, with the exception of the square miles in each Talook, which were obtained from the Civil Engineer, Lieutenant Bell, who informed me that they were carefully calculated from the areas of the several Talooks, according to boundaries laid down in the lithographed map of the Collectorate, from returns of the villages lying along the Talook boundaries supplied by the Mamlutdars, and that he believed them to be very nearly correct. The square miles, it will be understood, include the area of hills, rivers, roads, sites of villages, and all other kinds of unarable, in addition to the arable, surface :—

Talooks.	Number of villages in each Talook.			Population of each Talook according to Census of 1851.	Number of Square Miles in each Talook	Number of Inhabitants to each Square Mile.	Cultivation in the year 1850		Per Head of population.	
	Inhabited.	Uninhabited.	Total.				Beeghas.	Assessment after deducting remittances.	Beeghas in cultivation.	Assessment, Rupees.
Sowda........	98	38	136	59438	338	176	93796	187017	1·57	3·14
Yawul........	55	28	83	32394	280	116	57027	88542	1·76	2.73
Chopra....	98	104	202	33975	544	62	39208	76713	1·15	2.25
Thalnier.. ...	76	168	244	21026	898	23	30433	50189	1·44	2.38
Sooltanpoor.	327	124	451	36295	1312	28	71526	136282	1·97	3.75
Nusseerabad.	88	37	125	40290	288	140	86976	137167	2·15	3. 4
Errundole....	177	56	233	53592	336	160	96349	126783	1·79	2.36
Amulnier....	186	66	252	48032	530	91	96429	132194	2·	2.75
Nundoorbar.	232	84	316	53312	1118	48	89749	143526	1·68	2.69
Jamnier......	183	50	233	73381	568	129	140321	120433	1·91	1.64
Burgaon......	275	73	348	84044	822	102	144519	129382	1·71	1.53
Chaleesgam.	119	30	149	37110	608	61	49629	35259	1·33	0.95
Malligam....	190	14	204	60062	1120	54	115878	77963	1·92	1.29
Dhoolia... ...	159	66	225	59497	970	61	100346	82001	1·68	1.37
Pimpulnier..	211	128	339	33616	1270	26	44639	74775	1·32	2.22
Baglan... ...	284	13	279	39026	1076	55	99984	106167	1.69	1.79
Whole Province of Khandeish..	2758	1079	3837	785091	12078	65	1356681	1704392	1·72	2·17

" The actual area under cultivation in Khandeish is rather more than the beeghas recorded in this Table, as no allowance has been made for the extent of cultivation in certain of the wildest parts of the Collectorate, where the Revenue is collected by means of a plough-tax, and no record of the cultivation is made at all. A similar omission has been made in the case of alienated villages, but these are few in Khandeish, and the deficiency in the cultivated area shown in the Table due to both causes is not considerable.

" The beeghas given in the Table are all of the same size, and were obtained from the measurement of cultivation made for the purpose of settling the Jummabundee of 1850-51. The beegha contains 3,600 square yards, and is, therefore, almost exactly three-fourths of an acre. The begah measurement in Khandeish was never extended beyond the cultivation of each year, and therefore affords no data for ascertaining the extent of arable waste. When land once measured as cultivated falls waste, it is recorded thereafter as cultivable waste, but great doubt attaches to the area so recorded, from the want of any permanent boundaries to the fields, and the confusion of numbers in many instances. There is, besides, a large extent of arable land—probably upwards of one-half of the whole—which has never been under cultivation since we obtained the country, and is consequently not recorded at all.

"In preparing the following Table, which shows the extent of land in square miles, I have taken the beegha at three-fourths of an acre, and roughly guessed at the extent of unarable surface in each Talook, which I have deducted from the whole area to find the arable surface. The latter, of course, can only be viewed as a rough approximation to the truth; but still an approximation, even though not a close one, will give a general idea of the relative extent of arable, cultivated, and waste land.

Names of Talooks.	Total square miles in each Talook.	Deduct estimated extent of unarable hills, rivers, roads, sides of villages &c. square miles.	Remaining arable square miles.	Of which are Cultivated.		Waste.	
				Square miles.	Per cent.	Square miles.	Per cent.
Sowda	338	63	275	98	36	177	64
Yawal	280	40	240	60	25	180	75
Chopra	544	118	426	41	10	385	90
Thalnier	898	272	626	32	5	594	95
Sooltanpoor	1312	320	992	75	7	917	93
Nusseerabad	288	20	268	90	34	177	66
Errundole	336	24	312	100	32	212	68
Amulneir	530	45	485	100	21	385	79
Nundoorbar	1118	112	1006	94	9	912	91
Jamneir	568	40	528	146	28	382	72
Burgaon	822	70	752	151	20	601	80
Chaleesgaon	608	114	494	52	11	442	89
Dhoolia	970	181	789	105	13	684	87
Maligaon	1120	210	910	120	13	789	87
Pimpulneir	1270	348	922	47	5	875	95
Baglan	1076	326	750	104	14	646	86
Whole Collectorate	12078	2306	9772	1413	14	8359	86

"It appears, then, from the sixth column of the table, that the cultivated area throughout the Collectorate is only 14 per cent. of the whole arable area; while in particular Talooks, it is even more limited. In Chopra the land under cultivation is 10 per cent., in Nundoorbar, 9 per cent., in Sooltanpoor, 7 per cent., and in Thalneir and Pimpulneir only 5 per cent., of the arable area.

"Again, the great extent of waste, compared with cultivation, will be even more remarkable if we pursue the investigation into sub-divisions of a Talook and particular villages. The Talook of Sowda, as a whole, is the most densely peopled in the Collectorate, but notwithstanding that, it contains thirty-eight uninhabited villages, of which four are wholly uncultivated, exclusively of a desert tract about to be described.

"In this Talook, north of the Mahalkurry's station of Ravere, is a fertile valley within the Sautpoora Hills, which once contained a Cusba Town, called Pal, and numerous villages besides. These villages still exist in name, and the whole circle is called the Pal Tuppa, from the chief town of Pal. But the valley does not contain, I was told, a single permanent resident, and not an acre of the soil is cultivated. It is thickly overgrown with jungle, and infested by wild beasts. It is seldom visited except by Bheels and Brinjarries, who go there to cut wood and graze their cattle at particular seasons. In the neighbourhood of the sites of the old villages, mango and tamarind trees still flourish, and, along with numerous wells, attest, that at no very distant date, and probably within the last century, the valley was crowded with industrious husbandmen. The soil is described as most excellent, and some years ago an attempt was made, with the aid of considerable grants of Tuccavee from Government, to re-people the valley. A number of settlers went there, who cut down the jungle and ploughed and sowed a considerable extent of land. But the climate proved deadly in the extreme. The cultivators died or lost their health irrecoverably, from frequent attacks of jungle fever. The wild animals, especially the hog and neelgaee, which abound in the valley, ate down and destroyed the crops. After the lapse of a year or two a miserable emaciated remnant of the original settlers left the valley in despair, and never returned.

Such was the story of the Pal Tuppa as told to me, and I mention it thus in detail to illustrate the present state of the Province.

"The Pal Tuppa is an example of a once fertile and well-peopled, and doubtless, healthy tract of country having become covered with jungle and most malarious, owing to the destruction of the population during the anarchical times that preceded our conquest. It is by no means, however, the sole instance. The whole Ambeh Division of the Thalneir Talook is nearly in the same condition. The only inhabitants are a few Bheels, who subsist chiefly by wood cutting, and pay a plough-tax to Government for the few lands they cultivate; a division of the Chopra Talook, called the Dowla Turph, is in the same condition. Large tracts of Sooltanpoor, and the Nuwapoor, Mahalkurries Division, as well as other parts of the Pimpulneir Talook, are in the same state. The climate of all these parts is reported to be most unhealthy. The native inhabitants suffer annually from fever and ague, and from enlarged spleen. To those who are not natives the climate is still more deleterious, and it would be almost certain death to a European to remain for any considerable time in the jungles between September and February. They become less unhealthy as the hot season advances, but are never quite safe for Europeans, or even for natives unaccustomed to the climate. These tracts are, of course, very thinly peopled. The inhabitants are chiefly Bheels, who pay a light plough-tax, and cultivate as much land as they please. The annual Beghotee measurement has never been carried into these dreary wastes.

"Again, even in the comparatively well-peopled and healthy districts of the plain, large tracts of waste, extending for miles, sometimes without an intervening patch of cultivation, are to be met with. From the table following my 15th paragraph it will be seen that there is a considerable number of uninhabited villages in all the Talooks, and a large number of these are also uncultivated. But there is a still larger number of villages with only a very small population. Out of the 2,758 inhabited villages of the Collectorate, there are 587 with fewer than 50 inhabitants, and of these 181 have fewer than 20 inhabitants. In every such case the whole cultivation is confined to a few fields, and with this insignificant exception, the entire area of the village is waste and covered with jungle.

"To sum up these descriptions, we have, then, in Khandeish.

"1st. Large continuous tracts of jungle in the Talooks north of the Taptee, towards the Sautpoora range, and also in the western Talooks south of the Taptee, among the hills bordering the Dangs, which have a most unhealthy climate, and are either uninhabited, or contain a sparse population, chiefly of Bheels, who have not yet learned habits of steady industry, and to whose limited cultivation the Beghotee system of revenue management has not yet been extended.

"2nd. Large tracts are to be met with, even in the plain with very little cultivation, and with a very scanty population, uninhabited villages being numerous.

"3rd. In all parts of the Collectorate, excepting a limited portion of the eastern Talooks adjoining the Taptee waste land covered with thorn jungle far exceeds in extent the cultivated area; and villages with very few inhabitants or entirely deserted are common."—*Khandeish Report, pages* 1 to 6.

"The present dry-crop rates of Khandeish appear heavy as compared with the survey rates introduced into the Deccan and Southern Mahratta country. The highest, as will be seen from the statement following my 15th paragraph, is Rs. 2-10-0 per beegha, equivalent to Rs. 3-8-0 per acre. This rate obtains in Thalneir and Sooltanpoor, while the average rate of assessment on the whole land in cultivation in the Sowda, Chopra, and Sooltanpoor Talooks, is Rs. 1-15-0 per beegha, or Rs. 2-9-4 per acre. These rates could not be paid at all in the Deccan, but the superior fertility of the soil in Khandeish, and the ease with which its products can be converted into money, from nearly all being grown for export, as well as the advantages enjoyed by the cultivator in being allowed the privilege of free grazing over the vast waste of Khandeish, make them, in reality, far less onerous than would be supposed from simply comparing them with rates of dry-crop land elsewhere.

"The cultivators of Khandeish are, from all I could see and learn of their condition, in much more easy circumstances than those of the Deccan. They possess numbers of cattle which cost them positively nothing, owing to the abundant free pasturage. These provide more than sufficient bullocks for agricultural purposes, so that the cultivators have rarely occasion to purchase any except for drawing the Mohot, which in the case of the deep wells of the Taptee Talooks requires stronger cattle than are bred in Khandeish. Light two-bullock carts are to be found in great numbers in almost every village of Khandeish, and almost every cultivator possesses one more. In addition to these, the wealthier cultivators and the traders generally, keep light pleasure carts, in which they drive to market, or wherever they have occasion to go; and these little vehicles, drawn by fast-trotting bullocks, are met with in numbers on all the roads of Khandeish. The vast traffic passing through the province to Bombay, has, since the improvement of the Tul and Chandore Ghauts, brought a great accession of employment to the population of Khandeish. Independent of agriculture nearly all the carts used in bringing down cotton and other produce from Berar and Khandeish to Bhewndy belong to Khandeish, and are mostly owned by cultivators there. As soon as the harvest is got in, many of the cultivators either start off for Khamgaon, in Berar, or look about at home for a fare to Bhewndy, from which they seldom return with their carts empty. A trip of this kind occupies them about six weeks, and they usually net from 20 to 25 Rupees, clear of all expenses, if they are at all fortunate. Some of them make two trips before the rains. They are fast appropriating the traffic of the Brinjarries, and will doubtless succeed in doing so to a much greater extent, whenever the frightful and thoroughly-execrable road from the Tul Ghaut through the Conkan is superseded by such a road as has been made down the Ghaut itself—a measure which is urgently required for the accommodation of the vast and increasing traffic on the most important line of road in our presidency, with the single exception of that by the Bore Ghaut. In proof of the comparative abundance of money in Khandeish, I may also instance the fact that all labour there, agricultural as well as other, is paid for in cash, whereas in the Deccan and Southern Mahratta country agricultural labour is almost universally paid for in grain.

"These facts account for the cultivators of Khandeish being able to pay higher rates than elsewhere. But while fully admitting this, I am satisfied that the present rates are much too high, and, for the reasons already given, I am of opinion that a very liberal deduction is required."—*Ibid, pages* 13 *and* 14.

We must also quote the following for the sake of a few remarks which we shall subsequently have to make:—

"Population is, perhaps, already becoming redundant in parts of the Deccan, and low rates in Khandeish would probably bring settlers from it, and from the Nizam's Dominions, in considerable numbers. The collectorate of Rutnagherry is oppressed by an over-numerous and starving, but highly industrious, population; and could means be devised for systematically drafting off the excess to re-establish the deserted villages of Khandeish, Government might unhesitatingly venture to incur a considerable expenditure for this purpose in the prospect of a most ample return. The attempt would, no doubt, be attended with difficulties, but not such, I think, as are insuperable, and I throw out the suggestion as one which seems to me worthy of further examination."—*Khandeish Report, paragraph* 53.

"The suggestion in para. 53 of Captain Wingate's report, that the excess of population in Rütnagherry might be made available for supplying the defect in Khandeish, derives additional force from the description given in his report dated 30th January 1851, No. 44, on the Rutnagherry Collectorate, of the present depressed circumstances of the redundant population there. Among the causes which have led to the impoverishment of the people, he enumerates one which requires to be considered in the military department. Government here refer to the present system, by which, as they understand from Captain Wingate, recruits for the Bombay Army are drawn to a far less extent than formerly from the Bombay territories."—*Government Minute on the Khandeish Report.*

No. IV.

THE conclusion to all this will not be quite so brilliant as we should like to have made it We have been at some pains to inquire into the results of these, as they seem to us, admirable revenue arrangements, and a very difficult inquiry it is—the testimony on the subject being most annoyingly conflicting. The Maratha countrv. or at least the part of it in our possession; is much of it exceedingly barren,—perhaps the most sterile, after the great Ajmere desert, of any in India.

The population is too, industrially, an inferior one, accustomed formerly to eke out is own and its country's scanty productiveness by pay and plunder gained as soldiers and camp followers in other provinces of India. Under the Peishwas, says Mr. Elphinstone, there was scarcely a family of Maratha cultivators to be found which did not receive assistance from brothers or sons serving in the camps either as soldiers or as horsekeepers. We employ comparatively few soldiers, and take many of these from other provinces, especially from northern Hindustan, and the Maratha population is therefore thrown very much on its own resources. Then, again, their unthrifty and improvident habits throw them almost entirely for their capital into the hands of a race of foreign money-lenders—the Marwarries—who contrive, it is said, to make our civil courts the means of involving their debtors in much the same state of hopeless slavery to them, which, before the reduced and fixed assessment, they were in to the Government and its revenue officers. It has been frequently proposed, as a remedy for this, to revive the old system of *tuccavi* allowances, or advances of capital by the Government, who would thus, it is supposed, supersede the Marwarri money-lenders. Those, however, who understand the subject best appear to despair of ever preventing the jobbing and corruption to which such a system furnishes almost irresistible temptations. They believe too, that, with the present habits of the people, the Marwarri would still be resorted to, for expences incurred in marriages and caste feasts, —and they consider, certainly very justly, that the state of helpless tutelage, and childish reliance on his superiors, in which such a system places the cultivator, is precisely one of the worst of the evils from which it is hoped the improved revenue system may ultimately rescue him.

One bold and desperate looking remedy, which we have heard proposed by one of the greatest authorities in these matters, would simply have provoked a laugh in us, but for the very high opinion which we, in common we believe with all who know the proposer, entertain of his knowledge and experience in everything relating to the Deccan and its inhabitants, and of his usually cautious and sound habits of thought and judgment. He would force the most improvident of the ryots either into greater thriftiness, or into the abandonment of their holdings, by refusing all legal assistance in the recovery of debts, and so making it impossible for them to obtain credit. We do not know whether he proposes also that the Màratha peasantry should be allowed to repudiate what they at present owe. If not, and if legal assistance is to be rendered the money-lenders in recovering the present debts, and only denied them for the future, the first effect of such an enactment would probably be to sweep the country almost bare of its capital—the Marwarries hastening to call it in, and to transfer it to other provinces. Supposing then that repudiation is intended, since without it the measure would probably greatly aggravate the evil it was meant to cure, we fancy, that, while many Englishmen might not be sorry to see the sponge applied to the debts of the Maratha peasantry, could it be done entirely without our complicity, very few indeed would be found to desire that our Government should take any part in bringing it about; and we only mention the proposal to shew how widely spread, and how serious, the disease must be, when so experienced a revenue officer, and so careful and sound a thinker, can be driven to propose such a desperate remedy for it.

But to revert to our complaint of the contradictory nature of the testimony concerning the results of the new settlement. There are, we must tell our readers, two theories as to what the results of such a revenue settlement as we have been describing ought to be. The first,—the theory of Political Economists, of European thinkers and writers generally, and of the revenue officers who have had the direction of these recent surveys,—is amply and ably set forth in the reports from which we have made such copious extracts. According to this, *the moderate assessment* is necessary, to *enable* the cultivators to accumulate agricultural capital, and the *fixed tenure*, to *induce* him to do so. With a moderate assessment, the ryot perceives that he may, if he exerts himself, produce a surplus; while the fixed tenure assures him that he will be allowed to appropriate whatever he can make his ground produce beyond the moderate and fixed payment now demanded from him by the Government. He will therefore become industrious and thrifty —will add year by year to his stock, and, as this increases, will take more and more land into cultivation. The other we shall take the liberty to call the native theory, although it is held also by many of our own civilians—by those namely upon whom the lessons of Malthus or of Jones at Haileybury have made less impression than the suggestions either of the Dufterdars and Mamlutdars of their respective Zillahs, or of the native chiefs and Enamdars with whom they have been brought into contract. It was well summed up for us long ago by a very excellent man—a civilian too. "You know," said he, "the most intelligent natives always tell you, that the only way to make the Kunbi industrious is to screw him up with a good high assessment—that the lower you fix his assessment, the less he works." We have since heard the same doctrine maintained not only by native Jaghirdars, who might fancy themselves interested in maintaining it, but also by our own native revenue officers. And within the last few days a very intelligent native friend, who has recently, for the first time in his life, had occasion to study these matters practically, and the whole of whose previous training must have tended to prejudice him in favour of European views of the subject, writes to us from a Zillah in Gujerat.—"Nothing will ever improve the condition of this people till they are better educated. Since Mr. ——— was collector the assessment here is very moderate, yet the best judges are of opinion, that in the Guicowar's villages, where far more is extorted, the ryot contrives to produce so much more that he has just as much left for himself as he has with us." We attach no weight to our correspondent's testimony as to the facts in themselves, which—and we are sure that he would be the first to admit it—he can, as yet, have had no means of studying for himself; but we have no doubt that he re-produces very faithfully the opinion of the most intelligent people in that part of the country. Of course it is conceivable that this latter account of the people should be the correct one: nor are the two theories, at bottom, irreconcileably opposed to each other. Let us look for a moment at a somewhat similar instance. It is undoubtedly true that free labour is more productive than the labour of slaves. But it is true also, that since Hayti has ceased to be a country of slaves, it has ceased to be a conntry from which large supplies of Colonial produce are received, and that the diminution in its exports reprsents a real diminution in its productions. *And yet it is again true*, that if the Haytian negro is ever to be as productive as the workman of England or of Belgium, it wil lbe as a free workman, and not as a slave. And already there are happy proofs of his improvement in this respect. In comparisons between native states and our own, the balance of testimony we think is, that the native states are, *cœteris paribus*, more productive than ours. Whether this is really so or not, and, if so, whether it arises from the cultivator being, with us, left more to himself,—enjoying a liberty of action which, as yet, he is so foolish as to use to his own hurt, are questions which we shall not pretend to determine ; although we should wish to answer both of them, and especially the second, with a decided negative.

In the case of our new revenue settlements it would seem that all hypothetical speculation is a very idle employment of our time, since we have the facts themselves to appeal to. The Chandore report dates from 1840 ; and some of the settlements are still older. We have only then to inquire how in these districts they really have worked.

The facts, however, are more easily talked of than obtained, and verified. In the first place no natives that we have ever met with can be induced to acknowledge that the people in the districts with which they are acquainted are prospering. They may have many ways of accounting for it, each perhaps more stupidly absurd that the other.—With one the English are incessantly draining the country of its silver—the fact being that India imports far more silver than she exports. The tables of exports and imports abundantly shew this ; but it might easily have been anticipated. With their universal passion for hoarding wealth in the shape of ornaments, the Hindus are probably the greatest consumers of silver of any people in existence. Now whether they have any imports at all, will depend on whether they have anything to export to pay for them. But what the imports shall consist of will depend entirely on the national tastes. While, then, they have any exports for which they obtain a return—that is, while they have any exports at all, beyond those which go to pay our remittances, and to bring in our wine, beer, millinery, musical instruments, horses, carriages, saddlery, books, &c. &c., so long will the national demand which exists insure that a portion of the returns shall consist of silver. A lamentably large portion of the exports is made simply on our account, but there is, nevertheless, a large, and happily increasing, export trade, for which returns are obtained, to be consumed by the natives of the country; and there exists, therefore, and is likely to exist, an import trade in silver, as our Hindu friends may satisfy themselves by consulting the Custom House tables.

With another portion, incredibly stupid as it may seem, the distress is held to arise from the government not creating a sufficient number of places, and not paying the occupants of those which do exist sufficiently highly; such people of course imagining that the Government actually creates the wealth which it divides among the place-holders, instead of having first to wrest it all from the industrious classes. But this error is shared in by those even who ought to know better, and who, when they reflect, probably do know better. We were lately favoured with a persual of twenty-seven propositions for reforms in the Government of India, drawn up by some of the most intelligent young men in the presidency. With most of them we entirely agreed; but it was amusing to notice demands for sweeping diminutions of the revenue,—demands for a repeal of the salt tax, of the opium monopoly, of custom-house duties, followed, immediately, by others for measures which, to carry them out, would require that all the taxes in the country should be raised immediately fifty per cent.

There is one simple consideration which we wonder never occurs to those reformers who attribute the distress of the country chiefly to the amount of the Government revenue. This amount is twenty-three crores of rupees, a portion of which, too, is obtained from the Chinese by means of a monopoly price of opium. But, let us omit this, and take the whole twenty-three croses. Twenty-three crores, then, raised from say twelve crores of people. Now, on the most extravagant supposition, what part of this would it be possible to remit, and what effect could such a remission have on the general condition of the people? Could the most biting economy—could a committee of Joseph Humes—by any possibility strike off three crores of it? Was there ever a time when the whole revenue raised from the industrious classes of India was only twenty crores; or is it likely that there ever will be? But let us double the reduction—let us suppose that six crores are economised, and that the Indian Government is thus made the cheapest, in proportion to the extent of its dominions and the number of its subjects, which the world has ever seen; and what does it all amount to? A saving of eight annas per annum, or two-thirds of an anna per mensem for each individual! Let it be remembered, too, that the most philanthropic of political economists are compelled to admit that taxes have sometimes, even in England, stimulated the productiveness of the people—and that it is very widely believed among the most intelligent and best informed revenue servants, and by Europeans also, that our cultivators do exert themselves in some proportion to the severity of the assessment upon them, or to the severe means taken to enforce it, and it will be evident that it is only to the elevation of the *morale* of the people, to the growth of industrial ingenuity, and habits of thrift and foresight, that we can look for any improvement, and that reductions of revenue are of importance only from whatever tendency they may have, in particular cases, to promote such a change in the character of the population.

There is still, too, another most formidable subject to be considered. The new revenue settlement aims at producing, or at least tends to produce, something like a peasant proprietary. In the Deccan, probably, nothing else was possible. Now this is an institution, the merits and defects of which have been, and still are, very fiercely debated. The best English speculators have generally been opposed to it, although the greatest of living authorities, "the last and wisest of our political economists," certainly leans a good deal towards it—at all events to the extent of deprecating any violent attempts to abolish it where it already exists. One of the evils most dreaded from peasant property in land combined with the system of equal inheritance—and they of course will be combined here—is the excessive subdivision of the holdings, with the increase of population. The advocates of peasant property do not defend it from this imputation in any other way than by endeavouring to shew, from statistical returns, that the feeling of property brings with it feelings of prudence and foresight, and that while cottier tenants in Ireland formerly multiplied recklessly, peasant proprietors in France and Norway maintain an efficient check on their numbers. But who that knows the Hindu will venture to predict, for many a long year to come, the abolition of early and universal marriage; or dare to assign a date subsequent to which the Maratha peasant shall cease to involve himself recklessly in debts that hamper him for life, merely to marry his yet infant children? Religion, public opinion, his own notion of what is natural and proper, all urge him to it. A native laughs at you when you ask the question whether any change in the tenure of land would tend to check the custom of early marriage! And as to restraints on the principle of population, why half the consummations of marriages in this country are, almost literally, rapes committed on mere children.

In Kandeish, which the Pindarri and the Marhattâ so thoroughly ruined and depopulated, that after thirty-three years of peace and order there is still but fourteen per cent. of the arable land under cultivation, this may not become a practical question for several generations; but Rutnagheree, and some parts of the Deccan, already constitute another west of Ireland. Depopulating wars, and periodical famines, do not occur under our rule, nor do lands lie fallow for years, to yield, when subsequently cultivated, large returns to rude and unskilful husbandry; and the results are, that the habits with respect to population which suited well enough the centuries of anarchical rule, of wars, and frequent recurring famine and pestilence, which preceded our conquests, now threaten to flood some of the provinces with paupers.

Few people have reflected sufficiently on the extent of the change demanded from the natives by the enforced peace and order which we establish among them, and by the new principles of Government which we introduce. Let us suppose, that an inland Deccan province, growing only coarse agricultural produce, is to be regenerated by the means of a favourable land tenure, and consider what the steps are through which it has to pass. In the first place if there has previously been anything like actual coercion, if the revenue has been raised very much under the direction and superintendence of the revenue officers, these latter using occasionally rather sharp means to secure it,—it is quite possible that one of the uses to which the slave may turn his new found freedom will be, to indulge himself with a little idleness and recklessness. The Revenue Survey Commissioners do not, we believe, allow that this ever takes place. We have said quite enough in the early part of these articles to show that we entertain the very highest respect for these gentlemen—indeed, we think so highly both of their judgment, and of their extensive knowledge of the subject, that we should hesitate, on almost any amount of opposing testimony, to decide positively against them. We can only say that we have put the question to many observers—ranging in rank from the highest civilians to the lowest government karkoons, and that our informants are unanimous in their assertions that it does. We are anxious not to be misunderstood—whether such results ever occur or not, the experiment must be persevered in. The slave must be made free, if he is ever to acquire the valuable qualities of the free workman, just as a boy must be allowed to go into the water, if he is ever to learn to swim. Carlyle's proposed negro coercion, and the industrial regiments which he would have organised in Ireland merited, we believe, all the obloquy which they brought down upon their proposer. This transition state then, if it occur, must be patiently endured,—dealt with by whatever expedients may present themselves, and, if possible, got through with. Let us suppose it either never occurring, or happily passed over, and that the land settlement is producing the results anticipated from it. These are, an increase of agricultural capital and industry, and a consequent extension of cultivation. But an increase of agricultural produce, unless merely to the extent to which it may be actually eaten by the previously under-fed cultivator himself, will require an extended market—that is, a similar extension of all other industries to produce commodities to exchange for it. We shall otherwise have glutted markets, and grain rapidly sinking in value; and this has been a very common result of the establishment in previously disturbed provinces of our peace-preserving Government, and of the consequent extension of cultivation; and is one of the stock native grievances under our rule. With a versatile people,—having among them a variety of useful industries, and with no caste prejudices to prevent them from entering upon whichever of these promised to be most profitable,—the glutted market would, in time, cure itself. In such a community, the low value of corn implies a high value of all the commodities and services for which it is exchanged,—corn-growing is less, and all other employments (from the cheapness of food) are more remunerative than formerly. Corn growers or their children will be tempted to become artizans ; there will be a redistribution of the industry of the province; values will recover their old level, while everything will be produced and brought to market in greater abundance, and the people, of course, will be in better circumstances—circumstances better in precise proportion to the increase of industry which has taken place. But how difficult a process will all this be with a Hindu people; and there are absolutely no other means available. How much of starvation and misery will it require, to drive any considerable portion of a Brahmin cultivating population to become smiths, braziers, carpenters, weavers, leather dressers, potters, brick and tile makers, &c. &c. Why there are still distressed handloom weavers in Cumberland. And, moreover, it is to be observed, that we are by no means at the end of the difficulty yet, unless on the supposition that the Government takes its revenue in kind,—that its fixed assessment is a fixed quantity of produce per acre. This, as our readers are very well aware, is not the case; we take our revenue in money, and our assessment is a money assessment. Now the general increase of industry which we have supposed may very easily have been attended by a general lowering of prices, in which case it will have been becoming continually more and more difficult to pay even the reduced assessment. We shall have the case, a very common one in India, of a province, all of whose rude home products are cheap,—indeed, as the native tells you, a great deal too cheap, but in which no money is to be got. We are not then out of the difficulty, even when there has been sufficient versatility to distribute the increased productiveness of the people, in due proportions, over all the variety of industries they may practice, and so to restore the balance of *values*. With a money assessment, *prices* are also of vital importance. There must have been ingenuity enough to direct a sufficient proportion of the new industry to the production of exports—exports which shall bring in silver, and keep up the range of prices.

This then is a new, and by no means very easy condition, which, however, is absolutely essential to the permanent success of the settlement. The lowering of prices from the extension of cultivation and general industry, or from the extension of cultivation alone, has indeed usually its limit; but in an inland Deccan province, without navigable rivers, canals, or roads, and separated from foreign markets by ranges of rugged mountains, this limit is a frightfully low one. With no new exports, prices must fall, till the present produce of the country will bear the expence of the carriage to markets where money is to be obtained for it. And there are cases in which, were the produce given altogether gratuitously to the exporter, the mere carriage alone would make it unprofitable for him to take it to market. Colonel Sleeman relates an instance of a famine in a province near the Nerbudda in which corn could not be imported from a part of the country where it was to be had in abundance, since the Brinjarries and their bullocks ate it all in the course of the transit.

No. V.

The Indian Governments, it has been said, are eminently Governments of Record. A stock subject for facetious criticism in this country is the amount of foolscap and red-tape which must be expended before the hire of a couple of dhoolies, or the salary of a sweeper, can be finally sanctioned. Probably a good deal of stationery is wasted occasionally, but copious records are nevertheless excellent things when accurate information is required, when we wish to know which among the items that go to make up the prosperity of a province have been retrograding and which progressing, and are anxious to attribute these effects to the right causes, and in the right proportions. Loose indefinite talk, the result merely of vague impressions on the speaker's mind, or of his personal feelings, and of no accurate numerical knowledge, unsafe to reply upon as it every-where must be, is peculiarly so in this country. The Hindu in the Deccan, who is sufficiently intelligent to be a talker on such matters at all, will usually belong to the classes whose power and whose revenues have passed over to us since the conquest; so that, if even his national and caste predilections could fail to colour his vision, and to bias his judgment, the probabilities are that his tangible personal interests as a member of the formerly privileged classes have suffered too severely to allow him to be a correct observer, or an unprejudiced judge, of the changes in the condition of the other and larger classes of his countrymen.

The unanimous testimony of a class so situated, *if unsupported by authentic numerical statements*, is of almost no value whatever. Our intelligent and improving Young India party is by no means, as yet, sufficiently impressed with the importance of this consideration—they are hardly aware of the worthlessness of even the most honestly intended judgment when formed under the conditions we have described, and without statistical confirmation, or when gathered from the testimony of those whose opinions have been so formed.

This point is worth illustrating by an example.—The Hindus, as we have already said, universally believe that there is a constant drain of silver from their country. An Englishman, with them, is a man who comes out with a box-full of clothes, and goes home with a box-full of silver. The country is of course poor—it is always being drained of its money. Any moderately well-informed person, however, knows that a drain of silver—an excess of exports over imports—from a country which produces none, must be of very short duration; and accordingly our Hindu friends have only to consult the trade returns to see that not only is there no drain, but that, very much to the contrary, the excess of the receipts during the last five years into Bombay, over the payments to foreign countries, amounts (leaving England for the moment out of the question) to Rs. 7,44,50,172. During the same five years there have been both importations of silver from England and exportations to it, but, on the whole, the balance for the five years has been twenty-seven lakhs in favour of England. The final account then is

Excess of imports of silver into Bombay, omitting the account with England..Rs.	7,44,50,172
Balance paid to England...... ...... „	2,700,000
Total excess remaining...... ...... Rs.	71,750,172*

We do not attach all the importance to this silver question which the Hindus do, or we should be compelled to contend that so large an influx of bullion must be both a sign and a cause of rapidly increasing wealth. A very favourable symptom it certainly is, value it as lightly as one may. But the principal use we wish to make of it at present, is to shew how idly people must talk, who will not be at the pains to acquire accurate numerical information.

* Confining the calculations to the ports of Bombay, Guzerat, and the Concan, the absorption of silver in the five years is Rs. 5,24,98,369. Although silver is not, as so many of our Hindu friends imagine, the only wealth, nor its importation more a cause of wealth than the importation of any other commodity which the general public demand may make it profitable for the merchants to bring in; yet with the universal passion for ornaments made of it, which prevails, among the people, the imports of bullion are probably a rather delicate test of the command which they may at any time possess over commodities beyond the category of mere necessaries. Next to silver, copper probably among all foreign commodities, is the one, the consumption of which would best indicate the condition of the people. In ancient times, say the Hindus, the water pots were all of silver; they were subsequently, for many ages, of copper; but under the British, the people are so wretched, that the copper pots have every where vanished, and been replaced by earthen ones. Now the imports of copper during the first three years (the only years for which there are any published tables) are returned to the Custom House as of the following values:

	Rs.
Year ending July 31st 1849	19,18,299
„ „ „ „ 1850	29,56,703
„ „ „ „ 1851	39,10,599

We do not of course know the precise uses to which these rapidly

We have pressed this consideration on the attention of some of the members of one of our Young India political societies, and have been answered to the effect that they do fully appreciate statistical information; that they should be delighted to speak of the condition of the cultivating and labouring classes generally with the full

increasng imports of copper have been applied, but any hypothesis concerning them must be favourable. Let us suppose large quantities demanded for sheathing ships, or for making steam engine boilers, and we could hardly rejoice over it less than we should if it were all consumed in water pots. Our series of articles is more especially concerned with the Deccan, to which, of course the Concan ports are inlets ; we are bound therefore to add that the absorption of silver appears to be very much confined to the island itself of Bombay, and to Guzerat, and the countries which draw their supplies through Guzerat. Of copper, on the contrary, the Concan ports take their full share—the imports into them exceeding in value those into Guzerat, and amounting to considerably more than a fourth of the whole. Under the heads of sheathing and sheets, slabs and tiles, (all copper,) we have the following figures.

		Total Imports into Bombay.		Re-exported to Guzerat.		Re-exported to the Concan.	
		Cwts.	Rs.	Cwts.	Rs.	Cwts	Rs.
Year ending July 31st 1849..........	Sheathing and Sheets...	14,876	8,74,570	3,482	1,90,530	4,024	2,20,780
	Slabs and Tiles	8,197	40,5049	1,179	58,387	2,951	1,46,193
Year ending July 31st 1850..........	Sheathing and Sheets.......	31,316	17,09,924	6,917	3,74,592	8,266	4,38,565
	Slabs and Tiles	10,378	5,18,984	7,133	3,60,731	3,656	1,81,287
Year ending July 31st 1851..........	Sheathing and Sheets......	44,968	24,72,160	7,426	4,08,475	10,870	5,97,852
	Slabs and Tiles	13,473	6,73,[illegible]76	7,734	3,48,051	8,345	1,67,268
	Totals......	1,23,208	66,53,763	33.871	17,40,766	38,112	17,51,945

One of the first uses which a Hindu would make of returning prosperity would certainly be to put silver ornaments on his wife, and to replace the earthen waterpot on her head by a Copper one, and we cannot but think that these large and increasing imports of both metals must indicate a certain amount of improvement in the general condition of the people.

and accurate knowledge which authentic numerical returns would afford—but that these latter they have no means of arriving at; and that in pressing them for definite and accurate statements, in place of the mere echo which they now give of the, possibly very erroneous, common opinion, we are demanding bricks from them without straw. This answer, in the particular cases in question, is, we have no doubt, nearly correct. It only shews, however, how much progress the native community generally has yet to make, before it will be competent to any very useful discussion of political questions. The whole of the Government records, at some stage or other of the process of getting them up, pass through the hands of native officials. Much of the information contained it is not desired even should be kept secret, and it could not be kept so if it were; and yet the best informed and most intelligent Hindus can never cite a number from a tabular statement to support an assertion.

But to return. Let us suppose records, reports, and statistical tables open to us, and consider what point we should select as tests of the success of our revenue arrangements. We must beg our readers to allow us briefly to repeat the steps through which alone such success can be permanently obtained. The first is, that the low assessment and favourable tenure shall increase the means and the industry of the agricultural population, and lead, as a consequence, to a large extension of cultivation. The second is that the tendency of a large increase of agricultural produce to glut the markets, and produce falling values, shall act as an inducement to a portion of the cultivating class either to distribute themselves among other home employments, or to turn their attention to the production of exports—either agricultural or manufactured.

Of these two latter alternatives, the first—the increase of mere home industry—while it would of course add to the general abundance, would nevertheless be attended with a general fall of prices—rendering all fixed payments more and more onerous, and throwing a greater and greater proportion of the results of the industry of the producing classes into the hands of the Government; and of those who, from whatever cause, are enabled to command fixed money incomes. To maintain undiminished prices in the face of rapidly increasing production there can be, in the main, but one thing to look to, viz., an increase of the exports.*

The statements, then, which it would be desirable to have from our statisticians are evidently the following.

1st. Has the new settlement been followed by any extension of cultivation, and to what extent? If it has not, what are the obstacles?

---

* The subject of Roads, Navigable Canals, Improved Vehicles, and improved means of Transit generally, is thus intimately mixed up with the Revenue Settlement. Whatever, by cheapening the carriage, enables any product to be exported while yet at a better price than it would otherwise have to fall to before it could command a foreign market makes it more and more easy for the province to pay its fixed money rates in spite of an extending production. While on this subject we will diverge for a moment to ask—can it be that the best outcarriage for the Cotton and other products of Berar, and the middle and eastern parts of the Deccan, is to drag them up the slope of the country to the top of the Ghauts, and then down these hills, and through the rugged tract at their foot to Bombay? Is it not possible to command a much easier and cheaper water carriage *down the slope* to the Madras Coast?

2nd. Has there been a corresponding increase in other branches of production for the home market ?

3rd. What is the increase of exports from the districts to which the new settlement has been introduced ?

4th. What, since the introduction of the new settlement, has been the history of prices in the district ?

If the " Selections from the Records" are to be continued, we may perhaps hope, some day, to see these four questions fully and satisfactorily answered. In the meantime our readers must be content with the statements, which we shall lay before them in our next, and which are the best we have been able to obtain.

No. VI.

The Deccan Collectorates are Dharwar, Belgaon, Sholapore, Poona, Ahmednugger, and the Sub-Collectorate of Nassick. We shall commence our statistics with those of Poona. This Collectorate is divided into eight Talookas (or pergunnas); Sivnere, Indapore, Khair, Pàbhul, Poorundhur, Beemthurry, Havaily, and the Mavul.. The two last are remarkable,—the Havaily, as the district in which the city of *Poona, the old capital of the Peishwas, is situated,—and the Mavul, for having afforded to Shivaji the first and hardiest of his followers.

The four Talookas into which the new revenue settlement was first introduced are Indapore, Bheemthurry, Havaily and Pabhul; and concerning these we have the following information.

---

* Of the three conditions which, either together or separately, are essential to the existence of a large town; namely, that it shall possess peculiar manufacturing facilities—or peculiar facilities for the storing and exchanging of commodities,—or that it shall be the seat of the revenue consuming classes, the *nati consumere fruges*, Poona can pretend to the last alone. In a barren hilly tract, affording no materials for manufactures, and very ill situated for an emporium, it owed its advancement from a small village to a city of two hundred thousand people solely to the residence in it of the successive Peishwas; and on the downfall of their power would probably have shrunk gradually to its original dimensions. But the wreck of the Mahratta nobility, with such revenues as under us they were able to retain, still clung to it. We also made it our principal Civil and Military station in the Deccan, and discovered too that during the four rainy months it possessed a much more agreeable climate than that of Bombay. Its declension therefore has been arrested, and it is likely to continue to be a town of from seventy to a hundred thousand people.

STATEMENT SHEWING HOW THE CULTIVATION, ASSESSMENT, REMISSION, AND COLLECTIONS HAVE BEEN AFFECTED BY THE SURVEY SETTLEMENT, IN THE INDAPORE, BEEMTHURRY, HAVELEE, AND PABHOOL TALOOKAS OF THE POONA COLLECTORATE.

Name of Talook.	Number of Villages	YEARS.	Acres in Cultivation.	Assessment Rupees.	Deduct Remissions and uncollected balances.	Net amount of Collections.	Year in which Survey Assessment was introduced.
Indapoor....	75	Last of the Old Settlement preceding Survey ..	142,242	71,265	12,026	59,239	In 1836-37 in 29 Villages.
		1848-49, the last of the Survey entered in returns	219,468	74,251	572	73,679	1837-38 „ 46 „
		Increase attributable to Survey	77,226	2,986	„	14,440	
		Decrease „ „	„	„	11,454	„	75
Beemthurree ..	70	Last of the Old Settlement preceding Survey	94,203	75,173	19,708	55,465	In 1838-39 in 27 Villages.
		1848-49, the last of the Survey entered in returns	136,968	61,805	1,190	60,615	1839-40 „ 36 „
		Increase attributable to Survey	42,765	„	„	5,150	1840-41 „ 7 „
		Decrease „ „	„	13,368	18,518	„	70
Havelee..	66	Last of the Old Settlement preceding Survey ..	65,226	71,983	10,189	61,794	In 1841-42 in 46 Villages.
		1848-49, the last of the Survey entered in returns	85,790	58.692	38	58,654	1842-43 „ 15 „
		Increase attributable to Survey .. .	20,564	„	„	„	1843-44 „ 5 „
		Decrease „ „ ..	„	13,291	10.151	3,140	66
Pabhool....	57	Last of the Old Settlement preceding Survey	118,753	105,910	29,578	76,332	In 1841-42 in 25 Villages.
		1848-49, the last of the Survey entered in returns	157,430	92,242	11	92,231	1842-43 „ 25 „
		Increase attributable to Survey ..	38,677	„	„	15,899	1843-44 „ 6 „
		Decrease „ „	„	13,668	29,567	„	1844-45 „ 1 „
							57
Total......	268	Last of the Old Settlement preceding Survey ..	420.424	324,331	71,501	252,830	
		1848-49, the last of the Survey entered in returns	599,656	286,990	1,811	285,179	
		Increase attributable to Survey . ..	179,232	„	„	32,349	
		Decrease „ „	„	37,341	69,690	„	

Villages which had been alienated, and subsequently lapsed to our Government, are excluded from this statement. Those entered had been under our management for a long period previous to the introduction of the survey settlements. The comparison is made between the year immediately preceding the introduction of the survey assessment into each group of villages specified in the last column, and the year 1848-9, which is the last of the survey settlements for which the Commission has returns. The new assessments at this time had been from twelve to thirteen years in operation in Indapore, from nine to eleven years in Beemthurry, from six to eight in Havaily, and from five to eight in Pabhul. The comparison of the last year of the old settlement with the last of the new, is for the same villages in both cases. The increase and decrease of cultivation, assessment, &c. is shewn for each Talook, as well as for the whole 268 villages included in the statement.

The result, as our readers will see, is a large extension of cultivation consequent on the survey in all the Talooks; a great reduction of assessment per acre; a still more remarkable diminution of *unrecovered balances;* and *an increase of revenue.** The benefit to the agricultural country—*supposing prices not to have fallen*—is the produce of 179,232 acres of waste land brought into cultivation, in addition to the reduction of the assessment on all the land which they previously tilled; and the benefit to Government is a clear addition of Rs. 32,349 to the land revenue. *If prices have fallen,* and

* Save in the instance of Havaily, where the extension of cultivation has not yet entirely compensated for the great reduction in the rates.

unfortunately we have but little information on this head ; the Government gain something further by the increased value of money, as do, of course, all persons with fixed money incomes :—these gains being in diminution of those of the agriculturists.

This is, certainly in any case, a very successful result. It is clear, that either the cultivator, or the general community, has benefited very largely ; while the Government, so far from being a loser, has added a few thousand rupees to its revenue.

We must notice one more point connected with this table. So little do official people sometimes know of the business of their own office, and so unwilling is a Mahratta brahmin of the old school to believe that progress is possible under his new masters, that we had been assured by a very able native friend holding high office in our Revenue Department, that the increase of cultivation supposed to be consequent on the new settlement would be found to be entirely nominal, and to consist of alienated land lapsed to Government since the survey. We have succeeded in getting this point minutely enquired into, and have obtained the following result, which we have ample reason to believe is altogether unimpeachable,—namely, that, while the increase of cultivation subsequent to the introduction of the survey is, as we have already stated, 179,232 acres, the whole lapses for the same 268 villages, during the same time, amount to but acres 2,266. Not an acre of this enters into our returns ; but, had the error which our revenue friend imagined really occurred—had the whole of the lapsed land been entered as new cultivation, it would still have formed but a very insignificant fraction of the total increase.

The following table gives the proportion of the arable land in these districts now under cultivation :—

Talookas.	Number of Villages.	Arable land subject to Assessment.			Per Cent.	
		Acres in cultivation.	Acres waste.	Total Acres.	Cultivated	Waste.
Indapoor............	75	219,468	10,448	229,916	95·5	4·5
Beemthurree.......	70	136,968	74,289	211,207	64·8	85·2
Havelee...	66	85,790	8,560	94,850	90·9	9·1
Pabhool...	57	157,480	14,550	171,980	91·5	8·5
Total.	268	599,656	107,797	707,458	84.8	15·2

It will be seen that in Indapore the entire arable surface has been brought under the plough with the insignificant exception of 4½ per cent.—in all probability of wretchedly poor land, assessed at 1½ or two annas an acre. In Havaily and Pabhul more than 9-10ths of the whole surface is in cultivation. In Beemthurry alone is there any further room for much extension of cultivation. This district has suffered from a succession of disastrous seasons in which the crops failed extensively, and these misfortunes have greatly retarded its progress ; yet no inconsiderable degree of success has attended the settlement even there, the increase in acres under cultivation amounting to 42,765 on 94,203, and the revenue having been raised from 55 thousand to 60 thousand. A few good seasons in succession would no doubt bring up the cultivation in this district to a level with that of the others.

The only Talook, beside those mentioned in the statement, in which the survey has been for any considerable time in operation, is Poorundhur, and there it has been remarkably successful, although we have not yet been able to extract and reduce into shape the details concerning it. Beemthurry and a circle of lapsed villages called the Baramuti Kuriat, are the only parts of the Poona Collectorate in which the survey settlement has not led to the cultivation of nearly all the arable land, and to a considerable increase of revenue.

The following tables relate also to the same Talooks. We shall endeavour subsequently to bring the information they contain down to a later date.

LAND REVENUE OF THE DISTRICT OF POONA FOR EIGHT YEARS PRIOR TO AND EIGHT YEARS SUBSEQUENT TO THE NEW SURVEY AND ASSESSMENT.

YEARS.	Settlement of the year.			Actual collection of Land Tax.			Remissions granted.			Balance irrecoverable and struck off.		
INDAPOOR TALOOKA. *Prior to Survey.*												
1829-30	1,02,358	2	3	21,928	7	6	0	0	0	80,429	10	9
1830-31	63,805	15	10	14,941	2	8	0	0	0	48,864	13	2
1831-32	71,769	12	9	20,472	1	5	51,099	15	3	197	12	1
1832-33	74,034	0	10	17,019	0	5	56,832	1	5	182	15	0
1833-34	81,501	12	9	63,587	11	0	0	0	0	17,914	1	9
1834-35	69,600	13	4	61,679	9	4	6,081	6	3	1,839	13	9
1835-36	73,151	1	9	60,987	2	0	11,925	13	2	238	2	7
1836-37	73,212	0	4	67,392	3	3	5,702	2	0	117	11	1
	6,09,433	11	10	3,28,007	5	7	1,31,641	6	1	1,49,785	0	2
Subsequent to Survey.												
1837-38	73,091	9	8	68,918	15	0	4,125	3	8	47	7	0
1838-39	74,947	8	11	69,137	13	5	5,809	11	6	0	0	0
1839-40	76,864	3	6	72,756	4	11	3,447	15	2	659	15	5
1840-41	81,245	13	10	76,698	2	5	1,237	15	6	3,069	0	1
1841-42	79,710	12	6	70,934	7	3	739	1	11	0	0	0
1842-43	81,172	1	6	81,086	5	11	0	0	0	0	0	0
1843-44	79,149	14	0	78,719	8	1	161	6	5	0	0	0
1844-45	79,858	7	4	57,413	14	0	20,021	9	11	0	0	0
	6,26,040	7	3	5,75,665	2	0	43,543	0	1	3,776	6	6
TALOOKA BHEEMTHURRY. *Prior to Survey.*												
1829-30	68,984	7	8	29,200	4	4	39,027	3	4	757	0	0
1830-31	72,919	0	4	32,855	4	2	40,021	10	11	36	4	8
1831-32	66,862	2	8	41,070	1	1	25,750	5	0	41	5	11
1832-33	68,522	4	0	15,882	9	10	52,308	9	5	328	0	9
1833-34	78,565	0	11	76,212	12	1	0	0	0	2,352	2	11
1834-35	76,976	14	4	75,158	15	7	90	1	9	1,727	13	0
1835-36	76,268	12	9	63,656	2	8	11,442	5	5	1,165	4	8
1836-37	82,265	14	9	63,495	9	4	16,153	7	2	2,584	14	0
	5,91,359	9	5	3,97,531	11	1	1,84,793	11	0	8,992	13	11

Land Revenue of the District of Poona for Eight years prior to and Eight years subsequent to the New Survey and Assessment. *(Continued.)*

Years.	Settlement of the year.			Actual collection of Land Tax.			Remissions granted.			Balance irrecoverable and struck off.		
Talooka Bheemthurry *(continued.)*												
Subsequent to Survey.												
1838-39	73,910	10	4	57,122	7	8	16,774	11	2	0	0	0
1839-40	73,152	9	8	68,384	11	8	4,759	2	6	0	0	0
1840-41	74,951	8	4	7,335	5	2	1,574	9	5	41	4	10
1841-42	82,502	10	3	81,154	0	8	1,347	9	1	0	0	0
1842-43	87,332	6	1	87,332	6	1	0	0	0	0	0	0
1843-44	81,978	5	8	81,809	14	11	48	4	3	120	1	0
1844-45	80,158	7	5	55,495	7	0	21,962	13	0	0	0	0
1845-46	80,623	9	9	45,349	10	10	32,988	1	1	0	0	0
	6,34,610	3	6	5,49,974	0	0	79,455	3	6	161	5	10
Pabhool Talooka.												
Prior to Survey.												
1835-36	1,02,963	15	5	99,528	9	4	2,347	0	9	475	9	10
1836-37	1,00,461	0	4	78,130	7	9	21,219	9	11	660	15	1
1837-38	1,03,185	5	2	88,570	15	8	13,863	15	0	430	7	9
1838-39	1,01,567	9	0	75,908	15	6	25,470	12	7	62	7	1
1839-40	1,06,142	4	1	90,921	10	3	15,214	0	5	0	0	0
1840-41	1,10,844	15	7	77,655	14	8	33,183	11	10	0	0	0
	6,25,165	1	7	5,10,716	9	2	1,11,299	3	2	1,634	7	9
Subsequent to Survey.												
1841-42	1,01,768	2	9	88,828	10	8	12,916	13	10	8	0	0
1842-43	99,542	12	7	95,860	6	3	3,371	1	5	12	0	0
1843-44	99,985	5	3	99,456	10	6	511	2	4	0	0	0
1844-45	94,391	10	1	92,275	11	9	175	0	11	0	0	0
1845-46	97,433	0	2	97,426	0	2	0	0	0	0	0	0
1846-47	1,00,196	1	9	99,408	7	6	600	14	5	0	0	0
	5,93,317	0	7	5,73,255	14	10	17,583	0	11	20	0	0
Havailly Talooka.												
Prior to Survey.												
1835-36	97,766	4	10	84,715	10	10	1,653	3	7	9,299	13	5
1836-37	98,727	2	2	78,553	1	6	10,748	0	9	6,793	5	3
1837-38	96,015	1	7	77,794	0	7	12,076	1	0	4,901	1	10
1838-39	97,029	3	6	66,894	14	4	25,720	7	9	3,306	11	9
1839-40	1,00,208	15	5	78,661	1	9	20,700	2	8	467	12	5
1840-41	95,840	0	3	87,059	7	2	8,232	9	11	241	9	1
	5,85,586	11	9	4,73,688	4	8	79,130	8	8	25,008	5	9
Subsequent to Survey.												
1841-42	91,453	8	11	84,678	0	2	6,534	8	1	10	0	0
1842-43	85,133	11	7	83,096	6	3	1,767	4	0	5	0	0
1843-44	88,216	14	2	86,335	8	0	930	4	8	13	9	0
1844-45	94,487	1	6	93,326	9	10	99	7	6	0	0	0
1845-46	95,954	3	2	95,011	8	3	24	1	4	0	0	0
1846-47	99,180	1	11	86,734	4	1	17	0	0	0	0	0
	5,54,425	9	3	5,29,182	4	7	9,372	9	7	28	9	0

YEARS.	Settlement of the year.			Actual Collection of Land Tax.			Remissions granted.			Balance irrecoverable and struck off.		
ABSTRACT.												
Indapoor.												
Prior..................	6,09,433	11	10	3,28,007	5	7	1,31,641	6	1	1,49,785	0	2
Subsequent............	6,26,040	7	3	5,75,665	2	0	43,543	0	1	3,776	6	6
Increase Subsequent to Su vey.	16,606	11	5	2,47,657	12	5	0	0	0	0	0	0
Decrease Subsequent to do..................	0	0	0	0	0	0	88,098	6	0	1,46,008	9	8
Beemthurry												
Prior to Survey...	5,91,359	9	5	3,97,531	11	1	1,84,793	11	0	8,992	13	11
Subsequent to Survey .	6,34,610	3	6	5,49,974	0	0	79,455	3	6	161	5	10
Increase Subsequent to Survey..............	43,250	10	1	1,52,442	4	11	0	0	0	0	0	0
Decrease Subsequent to do.	0	0	0	0	0	0	1,05,338	7	6	8,831	8	1
Pabhool.												
Prior to Survey.........	6,25,165	1	7	5,10,716	8	2	1,11,299	3	2	1,634	7	9
Subsequent to Survey..	5,93,317	0	7	5,73,255	14	10	17,583	0	11	20	0	0
Increase Subsequent to Survey.	0	0	0	62,539	5	8	0	0	0	0	0	0
Decrease Subsequent to do.	31,848	1	0	0	0	0	93,716	2	3	1,614	7	9
Havailly.												
Prior to Survey........	5,85,586	11	9	4,78,688	4	8	79,130	9	8	25,003	5	9
Subsequent to Survey,..	5,54,425	9	8	5,29,182	4	7	9,372	9	7	28	9	0
Increase Subsequent to Survey.	0	0	0	55,408	15	11	0	0	0	0	0	0
Decrease do. do.	31,161	2	6	0	0	0	69,758	0	1	24,974	12	9
Total Prior to Survey...	24,11,545	2	7	17,09,943	14	6	5,06,864	13	11	1,85,415	11	7
Total Subsequent to Survey..............	24,08,393	4	7	22,28,077	5	5	1,49,953	14	1	3 986	5	4
Total Increase Subsequent to Survey...... ...	0	0	0	5,18,133	6	11	0	0	0	0	0	0
Total Decrease do. do.	3,151	14	0	0	0	0	3,56,910	15	10	1,81,429	6	3

Still more striking results will be brought out in some of the other Collectorates—especially in Dharwar, which is, too, in all respects, a very flourishing province. Also, in no Collectorate, we believe, will the results be inferior to those in Poona. And if we conceive the problem proposed to have been—to shew, that equalized and greatly reduced rates, with a liberal and fixed tenure, would lead to an increase of cultivation—an increase so extensive as completely to compensate the Government for its large remissions of revenue, we must admit that the extreme liberality of the settlement, and the skill and care with which it has been conducted, have been rewarded by the most entire success. If we enter upon the much larger question of the general progress of the people in industry and wealth, then, very satisfactory as this increase in agricultural industry is, we shall still, evidently, require to seek out answers to the three remaining questions in the list with which we concluded our fifth article; and these we must defer till our next appearance.

No. VII.

The accompanying Statements are intended to illustrate the working of the Survey Settlement in the Sub-Collectorate of Nassik.—

STATEMENTS OF CULTIVATION AND COLLECTIONS IN FAIR TALOOKS OF THE AHMEDNUGGUR COLLECTORATE, FOR SEVERAL YEARS SUBSEQUENT TO SURVEY CONTRASTED WITH THE AVERAGE CULTIVATION AND COLLECTIONS FOR THE PERIOD OF BRITISH RULE PRECEDING SURVEY SETTLEMENT.

Talooks.	Period.	Years.	Government Land. Cultivated. Acres.	Cultivated. Per cent of total arable acres.	Portion of assessment on cultivated acres collected, Rupees.	Average rate of collections on each cultivated acre. R.	A.	P.
Chandore. { Arable Acres by Survey......149,500 / Assessment do. 109,500	Prior to Survey.	Average of 23 years from 1818-19 to 1841-42.	81,200	54	92,000	1	2	2
	Subsequent to Survey.	1842—3	108,400	73	94,000	0	13	11
		1843—4	120,600	81	99,000	0	13	2
		1844—5	118,700	79	95,200	0	12	11
		1845—6	116,000	78	89,000	0	12	3
		1846—7	131,000	88	99,000	0	12	1
		1847—8	138,600	93	104,800	0	12	1
	Last year subsequent to Survey compared with average previous to Survey shews.	Increase......	57,400	39	12,800	.....		
		Decrease......	......	......	......	0	6	1
Wun Dindooree. { Arable Acres by Survey......102,300 / Assessment do. 76,000	Prior to Survey.	Average of 23 years from 1818-19 to 1841-42.	52,000	51	62,800	1	3	4
	Subsequent to Survey.	1842—3	74,000	72	63,800	0	13	8
		1843—4	68,000	66	63,500	0	14	11
		1844—5	66,000	65	61,000	0	14	9
		1845—6	67,600	66	62,000	0	14	8
		1846—7	72,500	71	64,600	0	14	8
		1847—8	76,000	74	66,500	0	14	0
	Last year subsequent to Survey compared with average previous to Survey shews.	Increase......	24,000	23	3,700	.....		
		Decrease......	......	......	......	0	5	4
Sinnur { Arable Acres by Survey......224,000 / Assessment do. 136,500	Prior to Survey.	Average of 25 years from 1818-19 to 1843-44.	104,000	46	114,000	1	1	6
	Subsequent to Survey.	1844—5	132,000	59	82,500	0	10	0
		1845—6	149,000	67	98,500	0	10	7
		1846—7	165,000	74	111,500	0	10	10
		1847—8	177,800	79	117,500	0	10	7
	Last year subsequent to Survey compared with average previous to Survey shews.	Increase......	73,800	33	3,500	......		
		Decrease......	......	.....	.....	0	6	11

Talooks.	Period.	Years.	Government Land. Cultivated. Acres.	Per cent of total arable acres.	Portion of assessment on cultivated acres collected, Rupees.	Average rate of collections on each cultivated acre. R.	A.	P.
Nassick. {Arable Acres by Survey.........105,500 {Assessment do. 81,500	Prior to Survey.	Average of 25 years from 1818-19 to 1843-44.	54,500	52	68,000	1	8	11
	Subsequent to Survey.	1844—5	55,500	53	52,000	0	14	11
		1845—6	62,500	59	58,500	0	14	11
		1846—7	74,000	71	65,500	0	14	2
		1847—8	80,000	76	69,000	0	13	9
	Last year subsequent to Survey compared with average previous to Survey shews.	Increase......	25,500	24	1,000		......	
		Decrease	......	......	......	0	6	2
Patoda. {Arable Acres by Survey.........329,000 {Assessment do. 162,000	Prior to Survey.	Average of 27 years from 1818-19 to 1845-46	129,000	39	109,000	0	13	6
	Subsequent to Survey.	1846—7	182,500	55	98,800	0	8	8
		1847—8	208,300	63	116,200	0	8	11
	Last year subsequent to Survey compared with average previous to Survey shews.	Increase.......	79,300	24	7,200		......	
		Decrease......	......	......	....	0	4	7
Five Talooks. {Arable Acres. {Assessment.	Prior to Survey.	General Average.	420,700	46	445,800	1	0	11
	Subsequent to Survey.	1847—8	680,700	75	474,000	0	11	2
	Last year subsequent to Survey compared with average previous to Survey shews.	Increase.......	260,000	29	28,200		......	
		Decrease.....	......	......	......	0	5	9

The Acres and Rupees entered in this Statement have been obtained by scale from the linear dimensions of a Diagram constructed to exhibit the results of the Survey Settlement, and they are probably therefore not absolutely correct, but yet sufficiently so to prevent the usefulness of the Statement being affected by any trifling inaccuracies in these items.

Taking Chandore from this as an example it will be seen that the average extent of cultivation prior to the settlement was somewhere about 81,000 acres, for which the rent paid was 92,000 Rupees, or rather more than a Rupee and two annas per acre. The first year of the new settlement sent up the cultivation to 109,000 acres, the rent for which at the new rates was, as will be seen, about 94,000 Rupees, being about 14$\frac{4}{5}$ annas per acre. The second year carries up the cultivation to 121,000 rupees, and the Revenue to 109,000 Rupees. There then occurs a re-action during two years, occasioned by bad seasons, the revenue falling, it will be seen, considerably more than the cultivation ; shewing that owing to the failure of the crops, remissions had to be granted, notwithstanding the reduced rates. After this both the cultivation and the revenue steadily progress, till but a fifteenth of the arable land is left untenanted. Our readers will readily trace for themselves the results of the settlement in the remaining talooks.

Our next tables will exhibit the working of the new revenue arrangements in the Collectorates of Sholapore and Dharwar.

Statement of Cultivation, Assessment, Collections, and Remissions and Balances for the several Talooks of the Sholapoor Collectorate, for Periods Prior and Subsequent to the Introduction of the Revised Survey Settlements.

MOHAL TALOOK.

Periods.	Years.	Number of Villages.	Government Land. Cultivated. Acres.	Per cent. of total arable Acres.	Assessment on Cultivation.	Portion of assessment collected.	Remaining on account of Remissions and Balances.
Prior to Survey.	1836-37 1837-38	59 2	65,541	43	53,651	49,871	3,780
	1837-38 1838-39	59 2	91,038	60	60,853	52,293	8,560
	1838-39 1839-40	59 2	95,888	63	59,493	49,959	9,534
Subsequent to Survey,	1839-40	59	1,03,891	70	44,062	37,702	6,360
	1840-41	61	1,20,935	77	50,718	50,538	180
	1841-42	61	1,33,720	86	54,267	53,623	644
	1842-43	63	1,42,863	87	57,571	57,496	75
	1843-44	62	1,35,447	86	53,895	51,291	2,604
	1844-45	62	1,36,526	86	54,030	54,030	0
	1845-46	61	1,42,426	91	55,966	50,692	5,274
	1846-47	61	1,45,496	94	56,959	56,941	18
	1847-48	61	1,49,332	96	58,189	58,179	10
	1848-49	61	1,47,083	95	57,396	57,396	0
Last year subsequent to Survey compared with last year previous to Survey shews an	Increase.		51,195	32	0	7,437	0
	Decrease		0	0	2,097	0	9,534

The increase of cultivation in the Mohal and Marha Talooks for the two last years of the period prior to Survey, is due to Waste land having been let out at the revised rates of assessment, and is therefore fairly ascribable to the Survey operations.

MARHA TALOOK,

Periods.	Years.	Number of Villages.	Government Land. Cultivated.	Per cent. of total arable acres	Assessment on Cultivation.	Portion of assessment collected.	Remaining on account of Remissions and Balances.
Prior to Survey.	1836-37 1839-40	68 3	131,175	59	91,720	81,297	10,423
	1837-38 1840-41	68 3	170,021	76	100,881	82,333	18,548
	1838-39 1841-42	68 3	185,575	83	102,313	78,523	23,790
Subsequent to Survey.	1839-40	68	1,97,198	90	76,710	69,300	7,410
	1840-1	68	2,07,468	94	79,719	79,340	379
	1841-2	68	2,11,008	96	80,805	80,274	531
	1842-3	71	2,19,355	96	83,489	83,135	354
	1843-4	71	204,212	90	78,064	77,934	130
	1844-5	71	1,97,659	87	76,080	76,064	16
	1845-6	71	210,665	93	80,739	63,878	16,861
	1846-7	71	2,16,178	95	82,485	80,465	2,020
	1847-8	71	218,524	96	83,359	83,329	30
	1848-9	71	214,772	95	82,233	82,233	0
Last year subsequent to Survey compared with last year previous to Survey shews an	Increase		29,197	12	0	3,710	0
	Decrease		0	0	20,080	0	23,790

KURMULLA TALOOK.

Periods.	Years.	Number of Villages.	Government Land. Cultivated. Acres.	Per cent. of total arable acres.	Assessment on cultivation.	Portion of assessment collected.	Remaining on account of Remission and Balances.
Prior to Survey.	1836-37 1839-40 1840-41	4 31 48	1,35,270	74	1,45,542	85,321	60,211
	1137-38 1840-41 1841-42	4 31 48	1,42,324	78	1,58,606	90,912	67,694
	1838-39 1841-42 1842-43	4 31 48	1,33,577	73	1,54,996	92,550	62,446
Subsequent to Survey.	1839-40	4	19,992	91	7,019	6,311	708
	1840-41	4	20,842	95	7,175	7,160	15
	1841-42	4	21,032	95	7,257	7,254	3
	1842-43	35	87,615	75	34,455	34,455	0
	1843-44	83	1,90,007	70	79,229	76,966	2,263
	1844-45	83	2,04,686	76	83,272	77,542	5,730
	1845-46	83	2,08,927	80	83,927	40,523	43,404
	1846-47	83	2,20,565	85	88,416	87,634	782
	1847-48	83	2,17,500	84	87,530	87,530	0
	1848-49	83	2,08,249	80	83,754	83,754	0
Last year subsequent to Survey compared with last year previous to Survey shews an	Increase		74,672	7	0	0	0
	Decrease		0	0	71,242	8,796	62,446

SHOLAPOOR TALOOK.

Period.	Years.	Number of Villages.	Government Land. Cultivated. Acres.	Per cent of total arable Acres	Assessment on Cultivation	Portion of assessment collected.	Remaining on account of Remissions and Balances.
Prior to Survey.	1837-38 1841-42 1842-43	108 1 9	1,94,777	61	1,30,155	115,205	14,950
	1838-39 1842-43 1843-44	108 1 9	1,99,100	62	1,30,102	119,489	10,613
	1839-40 1843-44 1844-45	108 1 9	2,55,303	80	1,50,817	1,42,422	8,395
Subsequent to Survey.	1839-40	0	0	0	0	0	0
	1840-41	108	2,48,739	84	1,10,676	1,06,459	4,217
	1841-42	108	2,71,373	91	1,16,173	1,13,542	2,631
	1842-43	108	2,72,857	92	1,14,851	1,14,643	208
	1843-44	108	2,60,040	88	1,10,709	1,10,566	143
	1844-45	109	2,64,125	86	1,15,911	1,15,900	11
	1845-46	118	3,08,435	89	1,33,531	1,32,907	624
	1846-47	118	3,23,420	93	1,39,898	1,39,898	0
	1847-48	118	3,22,972	93	1,40,060	1,40,060	0
	1848-49	118	3,16,236	91	1,37,135	1,37,135	0
Last year subsequent to Survey compared with last year previous to Survey shows an	Increase.		60,933	11	0	0	0
	Decrease		0	0	13,682	5,287	8,359

BARSEE TALOOK.

Period.	Years.	Number of Villages.	Government Land. Cultivated. Acres.	Per cent of total arable Acres	Assessment on Cultivation.	Portion of assessment collected.	Remaining on account of Remissions and Balances.
Prior to Survey.	1837-38	113	121,324	48	1,15,008	1,03,804	11,204
	1838-39	113	124,478	50	1,15,148	99,508	15,640
	1839-40	113	160,807	64	1,33,346	1,08,482	24,864
Subsequent to Survey.	1839-40	0	0	0	0	0	0
	1840-41	113	2,00,425	79	1,09,143	1,00,404	8,739
	1841-42	113	2,07,990	82	1,10,705	1,10,078	627
	1842-43	113	2,04,138	80	1,08,305	1,08,041	264
	1843-44	113	1,95,863	77	1,03,936	1,03,645	291
	1844-45	113	1,96,502	70	1,04,329	1,04,232	97
	1845-46	113	2,08,402	82	1,10,005	71,011	38,994
	1846-47	113	2,27,909	90	1,17,045	1,16,849	196
	1847-48	113	2,25,652	89	1,16,623	1,15,489	1,134
	1848-49	113	2,18,503	86	1,13,633	1,13,633	0
Last year subsequent to Survey compared with last year previous to Survey shews an	Increase.		57,696	22	0	5,151	0
	Decrease		0	0	19,713	0	24,864

INDEE TALOOK.

Period.	Years.	Number of Villages.	Government Land. Cultivated. Acres.	Per cent of total arable Acres	Assessment on Cultivation.	Portion of assessment collected.	Remaining on account of Remissions and Balances.
Prior to Survey.	1840-41 1841-42	46 76	2,11,068	60	97,240	93,981	3,259
	1841-42 1842-43	46 76	2,03,347	58	96,165	91,950	4,215
	1842-43 1843-44	46 76	2,01,691	56	85,650	80,553	5,097
Subsequent to Survey.	1839-40	0	0	0	0	0	0
	1840-41	0	0	0	0	0	0
	1841-42	0	0	0	0	0	0
	1842-43	0	0	0	0	0	0
	1843-44	46	79,835	49	39,529	27,922	11,607
	1844-45	122	2,08,590	55	98,577	77,829	20,748
	1845-46	122	1,90,300	50	91,344	71,661	19,683
	1846-47	122	2,06,625	56	97,612	96,303	1,309
	1847-48	122	2,26,397	61	1,04,657	103,929	728
	1848-49	122	2,40,518	64	1,08,093	107,408	685
Last year subsequent to Survey compared with last year previous to Survey shews an	Increase.	0	38,827	8	22,443	26,855	0
	Decrease	0	0	0	0	0	4,412

The acres for the period prior to Survey must be viewed merely as rough approximations obtained by converting the old land measures in which the cultivation was recorded into acres by calculation.

HYPERGA TALOOK.

Period.	Years.	Number of Villages.	Government Land: Cultivated: Acres.	Government Land: Cultivated: Per cent of total arable Acres	Government Land: Assessment on Cultivation.	Government Land: Portion of assessment collected.	Government Land: Remaining on account of Remissions and Balances.
Prior to Survey.	1840-41 1841-42	53 45	1,67,509	60	97,824	97,352	472
	1841-42 1842-43	53 45	1,48,374	53	88,801	78,664	10,137
	1842-43 1843-44	53 45	1,42,360	50	80,324	73,609	6,715
Subsequent to Survey.	1839-40	0	0	0	0	0	0
	1840-41	0	0	0	0	0	0
	1841-42	0	0	0	0	0	0
	1842-43	0	0	0	0	0	0
	1843-44	56	65,856	57	33,052	27,853	5,199
	1844-45	113	1,75,952	52	97,379	94,238	3,141
	1845-46	113	2,00,185	60	1,07,706	97,129	10,577
	1846-47	98	2,08,467	74	1,09,161	1,09,092	69
	1847-48	98	2,10,416	74	1,10,624	1,10,329	295
	1848-49	98	2,19,551	78	1,12,884	1,12,607	277
Last year subsequent to Survey compared with last year previous to Survey shews an	Increase.		77,191	28	32,560	38,998	0
	Decrease		0	0	0	0	6,438

The acres for the period prior to Survey must be viewed merely as rough approximations obtained by converting the old land measures in which the cultivation was been recorded into acres by calculation.

MUNGOLEE TALOOK.

Periods.	Years.	Number of villages.	Government Land.				
			Cultivated.				
			Acres.	Per cent. of total arable acres	Assessment on cultivation.	Portion of assessment collected.	Remaining on account of Remissions and Balances.
Prior to Survey.	1841-42	14	39,804	51	28,705	28,634	71
	1842-43	14	35,090	45	25,568	21,700	3,868
	1843-44	14	29,754	38	21,702	19,851	1,851
Subsequent to Survey	1839-40	0	0	0	0	0	0
	1840-41	0	0	0	0	0	0
	1841-42	0	0	0	0	0	0
	1842-43	0	0	0	0	0	0
	1843-44	0	0	0	0	0	0
	1844-45	64	1,05,735	57	64,945	56,408	8,537
	1845-46	64	1,07,423	58	66,852	56,235	10,617
	1846-47	14	52,066	70	32,922	32,656	266
	1847-48	14	55,500	75	34,191	34,191	0
	1848-49	14	59,628	80	36,152	35,749	403
Last year subsequent to Survey compared with last year previous to Survey shews an	Increase.		29,874	42	14,450	15,898	0
	Decrease		0	0	0	0	1,448

The acres for the period prior to Survey must be viewed merely as rough approximations obtained by converting the old land measures in which the cultivation was then recorded into acres by calculation.

MOODEBEHAL TALOOK.

Periods.	Years.	Number of villages.	Government Land. Cultivated. Acres.	Per cent. of total arable acres	Assessment on cultivation.	Portion of assessment collected.	Remaining on account of Remissions and Balances.
Prior to Survey.	1841-42	149	1,41,516	56	87,232	86,845	387
	1842-43	149	1,21,403	48	76,822	63,069	13,753
	1843-44	149	1,07,825	42	67,152	65,527	1,625
Subsequent to Survey.	1839-40	0	0	0	0	0	0
	1840-41	0	0	0	0	0	0
	1841-42	0	0	0	0	0	0
	1842-43	0	0	0	0	0	0
	1843-44	0	0	0	0	0	0
	1844-45	149	1,18,069	45	75,726	69,214	6,512
	1845-46	149	1,19,713	46	75,320	67,135	8,185
	1846-47	149	1,39,981	54	84,548	84,323	225
	1847-48	149	1,40,990	54	86,081	83,774	2,307
	1848-49	149	1,44,885	56	86,712	83,793	2,919
Last year subsequent to Survey compared with last year previous to Survey shews an	Increase.		37,060	14	19,560	266	1,294
	Decrease		0	0	0	0	0

The acres for the period prior to Survey must be viewed merely as rough approximations, obtained by converting the old measures in which the cultivation was then recorded into acres, by calculation.

ABSTRACT.

Periods.	Years.	Number of Villages.	Government Land. Cultivated. Acres.	Per cent. of total arable acres	Assessment on Cultivation.	Portion of assessment collected.	Remaining on account of Remissions and Balances.
Prior to Survey.		829	1,207,984	58	8,47,077	7,42,310	1,04,757
		829	1,235,175	59	8,52,946	6,99,918	1,53,028
		829	1,312,780	62	8,55,793	7,11,476	1,44,317
Subsequent to Survey.	1844-45	886	1,607,844	68	7,70,249	7,25,457	44,792
	1845-46	894	1,696,476	71	8,05,390	6,51,171	1,54,219
	1846-47	829	1,740,707	78	8,09,046	8,04,161	4,885
	1847-48	829	1,767,283	79	8,21,314	8,16,810	4,504
	1848-49	829	1,769,425	79	8,17,922	8,13,708	4,284
Last year subsequent to Survey compared with last year previous to Survey shews an	Increase.		4,56,645	17	0	1,02,232	0
	Decrease		0	0	37,801	0	1,40,033

For the 3 last years of the period subsequent to Survey, 65 villages, for which accounts for the period anterior to the Survey could not be obtained complete, are omitted, in order to facilitate a comparison of the two periods.

The crops failed extensively in the years 1844-45 and 1845-46, to which cause must be ascribed the large remissions and balances for those years.

STATEMENT OF CULTIVATION, ASSESSMENT, AND COLLECTIONS IN 1175 VILLAGES OF THE DHARWAR COLLECTORATE PREVIOUS, AND SUBSEQUENT TO, THE INTRODUCTION OF THE REVISED SURVEY.

Nature of Settlement.	Years.	128 Villages into which the new Survey Settlement was introduced in the years 1843-4 & 1844-5, viz. 80 villages of the Nuwulgoond Talook, & 48 villages of the Hoobulee Talook.				
		Number of Villages.	Land in cultivation exclusive of alienations.	Assessment of land in cultivation.	Collections on account of land in cultivation.	Collections on account of land of all kinds, waste and alienations included.
			Acres.	Rupees.	Rupees.	Rupees.
Previous to Survey.	Average of years preceding revised Survey Assessment.	128	1,65,068	2,13,840	1,66,410	2,39,967
	Year immediately preceding introduction of revised Assessment.	128	1,44,296	1,94,919	1,55,799	2,26,941
Subsequent to Survey.	1844-45	128	156,896	1,46,192	1,82,687	1,98,981
	1845-46	128	186,807	1,71,453	1,25,056	1,75,467
	1846-47	128	218,647	1,98,817	1,96,695	2,55,378
	1847-48	128	228,669	2,07,406	2,05,590	2,62,552
	1848-49	128	233,088	2,1[illegible],558	2,07,554	2,67,893
	1849 50	128	226.812	2,06,571	2,05,202	2,61,768
	1850-51	128	225,240	2,05,335	2,08,172	2,59,154
Settlement of 1850-51 or last year of revised Assessment compared with	Average of years preceding Survey exhibits	Increase.	60,172	0	86,762	19,187
		Decrease.	0	8,505	0	0
	Year immediately preceding introduction of revised Assessment exhibits	Increase.	80,944	10,416	47,373	32,213
		Decrease.	0	0	0	0

Nature of settlement.	Years.	86 Villages into which the new Survey Settlement was introduced in the year 1845-46, all the villages being in the Dumbul Talook.				
		Number of Villages	Land in cultivation, exclusive of alienations.	Assessment of land in cultivation.	Collections on account of land in cultivation.	Collections on account of land of all kinds, waste and alienations included.
			Acres.	Rupees.	Rupees.	Rupees.
Previous to Survey.	Average of years preceding revised Survey Assessment.	86	121,173	127,649	69,796	137,606
	Year immediately preceding introduction of revised Assessment.	86	138,291	146,960	103,435	141,336
Subsequent to Survey.	1844-5	0	0	0	0	0
	1845-6	86	151,287	95,515	59,273	80,093
	1846-7	86	172,588	107,625	100,091	128,484
	1847-8	86	174,012	108,494	101,934	129,253
	1848-9	86	18 ,500	112,662	105,145	132,505
	1849-50	86	176,497	109,055	102,457	128,291
	1850-51	86	178,098	109,525	102,133	127,386
Settlement of 1850-51 or last Year of revised Assessment compared with	Average of years preceding Survey exhibits.	Increase.	56,925	0	32,337	0
		Decrease.	0	18,124	0	10,220
	Year immediately preceding introduction of revised Assessment exhibits.	Increase.	39,807	0	0	0
		Decrease.	0	37,435	1,302	13,950

Nature of settlement.	Years.	137 Villages into which the new Survey Settlement was introduced in the year 1846-47, all the villages being in the Bunkapoor Talook.				
		Number of Villages	Land in cultivation exclusive of alienations.	Assessment of land in cultivation.	Collections on account of land in cultivation.	Collections on account of land of all kinds, waste and alienations included.
			Acres.	Rupees.	Rupees.	Rupees.
Previous to Survey.	Average of years preceding revised Survey Assessment.	137	76,048	129,264	88,113	138,453
	Year immediately preceding introduction of revised Assessment.	137	64,135	130,063	81,942	136,518
Subsequent to Survey.	1844-45	0	0	0	0	0
	1845-46	0	0	0	0	0
	1846-47	137	78,338	78,335	70,251	118,475
	1847-48	137	82,316	79,568	78,973	129,774
	1848-49	137	87,311	83,208	82,301	135,605
	1849 50	137	89,261	84,100	83,847	136,540
	1850-51	137	91,943	85,060	84,771	134,279
Settlement of 1850-51 or last year of revised Assessment compared with	Average of years preceding Survey exhibits.	Increase.	15,895	0	0	0
		Decrease.	0	44,204	3,343	4,174
	Year immediately preceding introduction of revised Assessment exhibits.	Increase.	27,808	0	2,828	0
		Decrease	0	45,003	0	2,239

Nature of Settlement.	Years.	845 Villages into which the new Survey Settlement was introduced in the year 1847-8, vizt 160 Villages of the Hangul Talook, 180 of Raneebednoor Talook, and 55 of the Hoobulee Talook.				
		Number of Villages	Land in cultivation exclusive of Alienations.	Assessment of land in cultivation.	Collections on account of land in cultivation.	Collections on account of land of all kinds, waste & alienations included.
			Acres.	Rupees.	Rupees.	Rupees.
Previous to Survey.	Average of years preceding revised Survey Assessment.	845	1,26,199	2,20,563	1,71,214	2,81,562
	Year immediately preceding introduction of revised Assessment.	845	1,03,729	2,28,468	1,54,140	2,61,805
Subsequent to Survey.	1844-45	0	0	0	0	0
	1845-46	0	0	0	0	0
	1846-47	0	0	0	0	0
	1847-48	845	1,28,073	1,68,506	1,34,588	2,33,092
	1848-49	845	1,49,598	1,55,857	1,48,472	2,60,976
	1849-50	845	1,64,622	1,68,880	1,67,906	2,69,070
	1850-51	845	1,67,941	1,70,299	1,68,992	2,66,248
Settlement of 1850-51 or last year of revised Assessment compared with	Average of years preceding Survey exhibits	Increase.	41,742	0	0	0
		Decrease.	0	50,264	2,222	15,814
	Year immediately preceding introduction of revised Assessment exhibits.	Increase.	64,212	0	14,852	4,443
		Decrease.	0	58,169	0	0

Nature of Settlement.	Years.	479 Villages into which the new Survey Settlement was introduced in the year 1848-49, viz. 134 Villages of the Dharwar Talook, 100 Villages of the Hoobulee Talook, and 245 of the Kode Talook.				
		Number of Villages	Land in cultivation exclusive of Alienations.	Assessment of land in cultivation.	Collections on account of land in cultivation.	Collections on account of land of all kinds, waste and alienations included.
			Acres.	Rupees.	Rupees.	Rupees.
Previous to Survey.	Average of years preceding revised Survey Assessment.	479	1,27,433	2,54,930	2,00,482	3,29,509
	Year immediately preceding introduction of revised Assessment.	479	1,25,111	2,58,545	2,14,043	3,58,440
Subsequent to Survey.	1844-45	0	0	0	0	0
	1845-46	0	0	0	0	0
	1846-47	0	0	0	0	0
	1847-48	0	0	0	0	0
	1848-49	479	1,53,812	1,74,394	1,74,319	3,07,940
	1849-50	479	1,97,008	2,20,831	2,19,190	3,47,118
	1850-51	479	2,05,096	2,25,101	2,22,927	3,51,346
Settlement of 1850-51 or last year of revised Assessment compared with	Average of Years preceding Survey exhibits.	Increase.	77,663	0	22,445	21,837
		Decrease.	0	29,829	0	0
	Year immediately preceding introduction of revised Assessment exhibits.	Increase.	79,985	0	8,884	0
		Decrease.	0	33,444	0	7,094

ABSTRACT.

Nature of Settlement.	Years.	Number of Villages.	Land in cultivation exclusive of alienations.	Assessment of land in cultivation.	Collections on account of land in cultivation.	Collections on account of land of all kinds, waste and alienations included.
Previous to Survey.	Average of years preceding revised Survey Assessment.	1175	Acres. 615,921	Rupees. 9,46,246	Rupees. 6,96,015	Rupees. 11,27,097
	Year immediately preceding introduction of revised Assessment.	1175	5,75,562	8,00,588	7,09,859	11,25,040
Subsequent to Survey.	1844-45	0	0	0	0	0
	1815-46	0	0	0	0	0
	1846-47	0	0	0	0	0
	1847-48	0	0	0	0	0
	1848-49	1,175	8,04,809	7,87,179	7,17.791	11,04,919
	1849-50	1,175	8,54,200	7,89,487	7,78,602	11,42,782
	1850-51	1,175	8,68,818	7,95,820	7,81,995	11,38,418
Settlement of 1850-51 or last year of revised Assessment compared with	Average of years preceding Survey exhibits.	Increase.	2,52,897	0	85,979	11,316
		Decrease.	0	1,50,926	0	0
	year immediately preceding introduction of revised Assessment exhibits.	Increase.	2,92,756	0	72,685	13,378
		Decrease.	0	167,246	0	0

Remarks.

1. No accounts shewing the "Assessment of land in cultivation" during the period previous to survey for "47 out of the 128 villages entered in the first division of the statement" being at hand, this item has been assumed by increasing the collections of the villages in question, in the same proportion that the assessment exceeded the collections in other villages of the Collectorate.

2. Accounts for the period preceding survey in the case of one of the 345 villages entered in the 3rd division of the statement are not at hand; and in this case the cultivation, assessment, and collections for the 1st year of the revised assessment, have been assumed to be also those of the preceding period in order to complete the statement.

3. The number of years included in the average for the period preceding survey, is not the same for all the villages entered in the statement, but generally exceeds twenty.

The total increase of cultivation subsequent to the survey as given by our tables is as follows:

		acres.
Poona	Collectorate............	179,232
Ahmednugger	do.	260,000
Sholapore	do.	456,645
Dharwar	do.	292,756
		1,188,633

And when to this we add the increase in surveyed talooks not included in our statements, together with the increase for years subsequent to the statements, we shall not perhaps much over-estimate the addition to the cultivation of the province if we take it at a million and a half of acres.

These, it must, we think, be admitted, are most satisfactory statements. The very great extension of cultivation which has followed the survey settlement is not, we believe, in all cases of quite as healthy a character as might be desired. The ryot has too frequently been tempted by the cheapness of land to extend his operations considerably beyond what the amount of his capital would fairly warrant, while his very defective agriculture, combined with this extension of cultivation, leads, it is to be feared, in some instances to a perceptible diminution of the fertility of the soil. But notwithstanding these drawbacks on the great success which our returns would otherwise indicate, it is not to be doubted that the quantity of agricultural produce raised in the Deccan has been largely augmented. This addition to the produce must clearly have benefited some class or other of the community. It has been either eaten by the ryots and the other previously under-fed classes, or hoarded as a provision for bad seasons.

It is not easy to get precise information on this head, but all our inquiries lead us to believe that it has been disposed of partly in both manners—that while the hoards of grain and other agricultural produce have largely increased, in (Poona and Ahmednuggur chiefly with the dealers—but in Dharwar to a great extent with the ryots also,) the cultivator has also been enabled to increase his own consumption and that of his dependants and his cattle. A full elucidation of this would evidently require that we possessed a history of prices for all the districts into which the survey settlement has been introduced; and this, unfortunately, we cannot obtain. Such information on the subject as we have been able to collect we propose to lay before our readers in a future number; and we will only here anticipate so far as to say, that such lists of prices as we have, do not appear to point to any general fall during the last fifteen years;—a time which covers the entire period of the survey operations.

Our readers will, no doubt, have been struck with the extreme lowness of the rates generally. The four Poona Talooks, with all the advantage of the lowest market for agricultural produce in the Deccan, pay an average rent, it will be seen, of only seven annas and seven pies, or something less than a shilling an acre! In the Indapore Talook the average is 8*d.* an acre!! In Dharwar the land of the best class, the famous black soil of India, that on which cotton is grown, pays on an average but 14 annas (1*s.* 9*d.*)—the rate for the most eligible portion of this again being but 1 rupee, 7 annas, and 9 pies, or something less than three shillings! What would an English, or even an Irish, farmer say to such rates as 8*d.* an acre for a whole district, or three shillings per acre for the best land to be had? The bold reduction of their demands to such rates as these reflects certainly the highest credit on the liberality of the Government, and one cannot but rejoice to see such a policy rewarded by an extension of agricultural industry, and the gradual restoration of the gross revenue to its former amount. But what volumes does the necessity for such rates tell of the wretched industrial character of the people, and their extreme unproductiveness. We must not, however, enter upon so large a subject as this at the end of an article, and defer it therefore till a future appearance.

No. VIII.

In concluding our last article we glanced at the fabulously low rates at which land is obtained under the new settlement. An average for the whole Talooka of Indapore of 5 annas 3 pies (about 8d.) per acre—for the four oldest surveyed districts of the Poona Collectorate (one of them containing the large and rich market of Poonah) 7 annas 7 pies (1s.)—for the Dharwar black cotton soil 14as. (1s. 9d.) Nor is this, we think, the result of an excessive and mistaken liberality on the part of the Assessors and the Government. The large remissions which have to be granted every year in unsurveyed districts; the frequent complaints, in the annual reports of the Revenue authorities, of the poverty of the people; the great stimulus to agriculture which the new settlement, with its reduced rates, invariably gives; and the much greater ease with which the Revenue has been hitherto collected under it, all show that the relief was really needed. The average rents realized from the land under cultivation are of course immediately obtainable from the Revenue returns. The average value of the produce there are, we fear, no means of arriving at. A Revenue Officer, the most competent probably of any in the Presidency to form a guess on the subject, wishing to make a rough estimate of the value of the produce brought into existence by the extension of cultivation under the new settlement, took it, we remember, at two rupees an acre—doubting, at the same time, whether this was not rather too low. Let us suppose it then 2½ rupees, or 5s. (making the Government demand, at present prices, about, perhaps, one-fourth of the gross value,) and what would—not Mr. Mechi, or the farmers of the Carse of Gowrie,—but the most slovenly Irish cottier, think of such an absurd return from the land as this? It may be said, perhaps, that this is not so much from defective agriculture as from the want of markets for the produce. But, even then, how helpless, how resourceless a population, which can neither create a miscellaneous home industry to constitute a market for its agricultural products, nor produce anything on its soil which will bear the expense of carriage to markets where money is abundant, and fair prices are obtainable.

Liberal and admirable a measure as the new settlement is, and essential as it undoubtedly was, as the first step towards any improvement in the province, it is clear that something much greater still remains to be accomplished. It is altogether impossible that a people raising merely bulky and coarse agricultural produce should ever be able to pay a money revenue of any amount; and not only so, but they themselves, however liberally treated, can never be otherwise than wretchedly poor,—in favourable seasons living perhaps in rude and course abundance, but reduced to poverty and distress at the occurrence of every unfavourable one.

The great desiderata are more varieties of industry, and, above all things, more eligible and more abundant exports. Under our rule an unheard-of portion of the Revenue of the country is spent for foreign commodities. A Governor, a Member of Council, a Judge, or a Collector does not, as a native Rajah or Jaghirdar would, spend his income on crowds of retainers and hangers on of all kinds, creating a large demand for bajree, jowaree, ghee, and goor—he requires Long-Acre carriages, Arabian horses, French and Spanish wines, Parisian and London millinery, and a long list of foreign etceteras. The rich native also now imitates him in almost all these things, and even the comparatively poor one expends whatever revenue he may have, beyond what is just sufficient to supply him with necessaries, in English cloth and copper, and China silver and silk. This intense demand for foreign commodities renders it of vital importance that the experts which are to pay for them, and to provide also, if we are considering the case of all India, for the large tribute which in various shapes we exact, but of which the Deccan probably pays no portion whatever, should be such as are in their turn greatly in demand among foreigners, and contain considerable value in small bulk, so as to be easily and cheaply transported. Our rule will be light or heavy in India, almost in exact proportion to the facility, or the difficulty, which the country has in creating a demand abroad for its products.

Let us suppose a native prince and nobility such as Bajirao and the Mahratta sirdars were to suddenly change their tastes and habits, to dismiss the swarms of brahmins hanging about them, and the suwars, peons, ghorawallas, and troops of idle servants, to whose maintenance their revenues had hitherto been devoted, to keep but few horses, and these purchased from the Persian Gulf instead of from the valley of the Bheemthurry, and to spend, as we do, the revenues which supported all these dependants in every variety of foreign luxury. The first effect, evidently, must be great misery to the classes thus deprived of their accustomed means of living; the second, that the money no longer finding its way through these to the grain and other provision dealers, and through them to the producers, these latter will not have it to return to their rulers as revenue; there will be a general inability to pay the former rates for land, and every symptom of poverty and distress. In the mean time the foreign luxuries in question being at first paid for in silver, the drain of this from the province will have produced falling prices. When these have fallen low enough to make it profitable to export the rude produce of the country, the drain will stop, and the foreign goods be henceforth paid for by these greatly deteriorated products.

If we now wish to follow the fates of the unproductive classes, which this change has thrown upon their own resources, we shall probably find that some of them have migrated, and left the province altogether, that some hang on still in a state of poverty, depending perhaps on relations much less able than formerly to assist them, and that some probably resort to the land, forcing, in so doing, increased supplies of grain on a market in which the demand is already greatly diminished.

But is it then an evil to compel swarms of idle unproductive people to seek to earn their living by agriculture, trade, or some other kind of productive industry? And is it not demonstrable that foreign goods, although for a short time paid for by money, are, in all cases where the trade continues, ultimately exchanged against goods, so that the spending with the foreigner resolves itself into—not a destruction of home industry—but a mere change in the kind of it ? And does not all progress in wealth, on the part of a community, necessitate a constant redistribution of employments—a redistribution which will only take place, usually, under the pressure of necessity, and which implies in almost every case either some amount of suffering, or, at best, of anxiety and inconvenience ? We will answer these questions by a reference to the case under discussion—that of the Deccan, or any similar native province. What change then in the industry of the people would these new circumstances, this change in the habits and tastes of their rulers, and in the manner in which these latter chose to consume their revenues, require, in order that it should all take place without suffering and distress ? The dismissed retainers must evidently become productive workers of some sort or other. The completest arrangement would be, that they should become producers of precisely the things which the new tastes of their masters demanded. But could they even be gifted by a sudden inspiration with the skill and industrial habits necessary for this, there would still be something more required. In buying from the foreigner it is not merely his skill and industry that we pay him for : we have also either to replace or to remunerate him for the use of his varied and frequently gigantic capital. That portion of it which consists in mere labourer's necessaries is, of course, already in existence in the province ; but all the remainder, the tools, machines, and all the varied list of materials, would require to be suddenly created in addition to the new skill and new habits of industry. How utopian a dream this is, we need not pause to point out. We shall leave it, and pass over also many hypotheses that might be framed, to come at once to the simplest and most practicable of them all. Our population of unemployed retainers will, many of them, know something about tillage, and, if they could become industrial producers at all, could probably most readily do so as cultivators. This, as we have so amply seen, would by no means necessarily be any improvement ; it might, as we have shewn, only add to the embarrassment, by adding to an industry already fully supplied, and accelerating, rather than retarding, the downfall of prices. To meet our case completely, the industry, of whatever kind it may be, must provide exports which shall pay for the new imports, without the necessity of the great fall of prices necessary to send the grain of the country abroad. If agricultural then, or semi-agricultural, it must consist in the production of such valuable products as opium, sugar, spirits, indigo, cochineal, cotton, silk, wool, tobacco, &c. ; and could the skill and capital required for the production of such commodities as these be suddenly imparted to the idle classes, such a change as we have supposed would not inflict either loss or suffering on the province, the imports being in that case virtually a new creation of wealth, the result of the new industry of the classes in question. These would in fact supply to their rulers the imports, (obtained in exchange for their newly raised exports,) in the place of the unproductive services which they formerly rendered; receiving, as they formerly did, the rulers' revenue in payment, and spending it, as they had hitherto done, with the banyan dealers, through whom it passes to the ordinary cultivators, to be again paid in undiminished rents to the landlord, the state.

This is but a very rough sketch, omitting much that would belong to the actual working of such a state of industry, although including all that is essential to our present argument. The one point to bring out is the importance, both to the Government and the people, of the production of exports. The simplest change which could be brought about,—the variety of industry which, as resembling most nearly what he already practices, the ryot would most easily fall into,—is the raising of commodities for the foreign market *from the soil.* The Hindu is now known to be much more docile than was formerly believed, and we cannot help thinking that something like the agricultural schools, model farms, and itinerant agricultural teaching which have lately been doing so much good in Ireland, some adaptation of them suitable to India, would not be found beyond the power of our Revenue Secretary and Revenue survey officers to bring into existence. The successful introduction of an export which should bring money into the province, and raise general prices to the extent of only one shilling on each acre of produce, would be a second boon almost as great as that of the revenue settlement itself, and would richly pay for much unsuccessful, or partially successful, previous experimenting. We do not think that any unfavourable augury is to be drawn from the little success which has attended some of the ill-conceived experiments to improve the products of the province which have already been made. Where the Grant Medical College, the Elphinstone Institution, and the Poonah College succeed, we do not see why an agricultural school, if attempted with all the light on the subject which may now be obtained from home, need be under much apprehension of failure.

No. IX.

The accompanying letter on the subject of these papers will, we think, be found interesting. Some of the italics are our own, as is also a note to the portion of it which treats of the Cotton cultivation. The letter is in answer to a number of queries, some of which are given with the answers ; the remainder our readers must infer from the tenor of the replies to them. The writer will, we hope, excuse the use we make of his communication.

19*th July*, 1852.

I have just received your's of Tuesday last, and lose no time in replying to your queries, to the best of my ability.

1. Why are Nuggur and Poona so much behind Dharwar? Is the Dharwar population a better one? Is the land more fertile? Is the population less dense in proportion to the productiveness of the land? Did they start with more capital, and if so, how obtained?

Chiefly owing to the character of the population and the climate, Nuggur and Poona are wholly Mahratta, and the Mahratta cultivators, as I told you before, are ignorant, lazy, improvident, and deceitful. They are no match in intelligence for the money-loving Marwarrees, and fall an easy prey to them. The climate is subject to droughts, and the crops, in consequence, to frequent and extensive failures, when a large portion of the agricultural capital is generally swept away. This uncertainty of climate and the calamitous losses it occasions to the cultivators, which no forethought on their part can avert, has probably had a large share in making the character of the population what it is. In Dharwar the fall of rain is much more certain, and the crops less liable to failure. They are also, from the same cause, generally much heavier. The yield per acre, on the average, is more in Dharwar than in Poona or Nuggur, on soils of equal natural fertility. The Dharwar population is a greatly better one. The cultivators are chiefly Lingayuts, and, as a class, are intelligent and frugal, except on great occasions, such as marriages, &c., and with a keen love for money and great aptitude for trading. Many of them lend money to their poorer neighbours, and in addition to their agricultural operations take up the trade of the Marwarree in the Deccan, besides. They are speculative, and far less wedded to old customs than the ignorant prejudiced Coonbee, and have little hesitation in striking into a new path if it promises to lead to profit. Witness the New Orleans Cotton, of which more anon. The bankers and great traders are almost universally natives of the country, and generally Lingayuts or Brahmins. They too are much more versatile and large-hearted than the same class in the Deccan. There are a few Goozurs and Marwarrees, but very few ; and none of the hungry adventurers that troop down from the Northern Provinces to fleece the poor Deccanees can find victims here. The frugal profit-seeking Lingayuts have too keen an eye to business, and are not to be done. The great traders and bankers have speculated largely in agricultural produce, since the introduction of the new settlements, and keenly compete with the agents of the Bombay native houses who come up, or rather are permanently stationed, here for the purpose of purchasing cotton and other produce for the Bombay Market.

As an instance I may mention———— of Gudduck, a small agricultural town, about 40 miles from Dharwar, who died last month, leaving a fortune of 9 lacs of rupees, of which the better half is said to have been made within the last five or six years, by fortunate speculations in cotton, *i. e.*, since the survey settlements gave the great stimulus to the extension of the cultivation of the crop. He contracted with the cultivators for the crop at a certain price, and made them advances of capital to enable them to grow it. The same course was followed by hundreds of others; and the hoards of these Sowkars, which before the new settlement had lain unproductive in the shape of coin and jewels, were, on the reduction of assessment, drawn forth and applied to agriculture. I have no doubt whatever that a very large amount of hoarded unproductive capital was liberated in this way by the introduction of the new settlements. I know of many instances of it myself, and have no reason for believing that such instances were at all exceptional.

However this may be, by far the greatest effect has been produced by accumulations of capital by the farmers themselves, consequent on the greater profits obtained under the new settlements. These accumulations in the aggregate are, I am certain, from personal observation and enquiry, quite enormous. From the improved cultivation of this Collectorate, the many improvements such as the conversion of dry crop land into rice land, the construction and repair of small tanks by the cultivators, the planting of trees, the building of houses, the purchase of carts, &c. of which evidences meet the eye at every turn, I am quite satisfied that I do not overstate the fact in saying that the capital now employed in agriculture is double what it was eight years ago, when the first survey settlement was made.* The success of the settlements in Dharwar has gone beyond my most sanguine expectations, and it really would be difficult to paint it in too high colors. The population in Dharwar is, I think, less dense than in Poona and Nuggur in proportion to the productiveness of the land; but not very much so. Prices are much lower here than in the Deccan or Khandeish, *i. e.*, prices of grain; but cotton and chillies are exported largely from the Collectorate, which are hardly grown at all in the Deccan, besides other products; so that there is no want of a market; and nothing like a glut of agricultural products has been occasioned by the vast extension of cultivation that has taken place under the new settlements.

The same is the case in Poona and Nuggur. Prices every where in the surveyed districts I believe to be as high, or higher, now, than when the settlements were first introduced, which is to be accounted for by the large exports. The valley of the Godaveree exports grain to Bombay, Poona, and Khandeish to a large extent. Prices of grain, in Khandeish are generally higher than in the adjoining districts of Nuggur, owing to the former not producing grain sufficient for its own consumption, and

* Floating capital that is; and not wells, tanks and such permanent improvements.

consequently there is a considerable import of grain into Khandeish from the Deccan. Khandeish has at all times been a large exporting province, and in former times to a vastly greater extent than now. There was an immense export of indigo at one time, and a great part of the Peninsula seems to have been supplied with this dye from the province, in addition to large exports to foreign countries from the port of Surat. The cultivation of indigo has declined rapidly of late years, and is now almost abandoned, which is to be ascribed to the indigo now so largely produced by the Bengal planters being of superior quality, and to cotton having become a more profitable crop.

The great extension of cultivation *immediately* following the introduction of the new settlements, I ascribe chiefly to over-speculation in land. Every body fancies that everybody else wants the particular field he does, and rushes to secure it without duly weighing the cost. He begins to find out that he would have done better to have been less hasty in extending his farm, and hence, in some districts, a partial subsequent collapse.

Another cause of slight collapses in the Deccan has been unfavourable seasons of late years, in a good many of the surveyed districts; another, in the Deccan especially, is the exhaustion of the very poor soils which have been very largely taken into cultivation under the new settlements. After six or seven years continuous cropping, the return becomes very small, and they are relinquished, in many instances. But capital again accumulates, and I anticipate that a more steady increase of cultivation will everywhere follow the collapse, and that the cultivation will attain a mean maximum elevation, about which it will oscillate according to the seasons. This point has been attained, I think, in the early settled villages of Indapoor, and in the Nuvulgoond Talook of Dharwar, which was the first settled. In the latter, cultivation has been carried to a point wholly unprecedented, and I have just been told by Mr.—, the Assistant Collector in charge, that the assessment of the whole waste only amounts to 1,100 rupees, *which is the whole amount unrealized out of a maximum rental of* 2½ *lacs!* I do not exactly know the number of acres waste, but it can hardly exceed 1 or 2 per cent. of the arable area.

The progress of the New Orleans cotton-cultivation for the last four years is entirely spontaneous, and the following statistics of both it and the native cotton grown in this Collectorate, may be interesting :—

Years.	Acres Cultivated. New Orleans.	Native	Total. Acres.	
1843-4	545	178,411	178,956	
1844-5	2,749	182,337	185,086	
1845-6	11,176	164,591	175,567	
1846-7	22,329	159,498	181,827	
1847-8	20,499	182,888	203,387	
*1848-9	3,237	201,579	204,925	
1849-50	15,396	225,685	240,081	Part of the increase of native cotton in these years is due to the villages of the Moolgoond Mahal having lapsed to Govt.
1850-51	31,172	228,807	259,979	
1851-52	42,647	221,676	264,323	

This brings down the account of the New Orleans a year later than your statistics, and exhibits the same astonishing extension of the culture. Up to 1847-48 the forcing system prevailed, and had apparently reached its limit, as the cultivators were getting fast disgusted with the whole business, which is pretty* well shewn by the collapse from 20,000 acres to 3,000 acres in the following year when the local officers gave up interference altogether. From that time a healthy natural extension took place, and in four years the cultivation is double what it attained under the fostering system. The survey settlement of Nuvulgoond, a great cotton district, was made in 1844-5, and the increase in the cotton cultivation in that and subsequent years is attributable to the survey settlements.

I believe you have correctly inferred the increase of the imports of copper into the Conkan ports to be an indication of the improved condition of the people of our own districts. The imports

* "One or two unfavourable seasons, added to the indiscreet interference of the village officers, have lately had the effect of producing a disinclination among the ryots to undertake the cultivation of the new Orleans species of cotton."—*Annual Report from the Collector for the year* 1847-48.

must either have been consumed by them or by the Nizam's subjects, and from all accounts I should conclude the consumption of the latter to be falling off, rather than on the increase, in the cases of copper and all other imports.

I have omitted to mention above that it may seem to require explanation that a *greater extension* of cotton culture than shewn in my table has not taken place under the survey settlements. I am satisfied myself that a much greater extension is possible, *so far as suitable soils are concerned*, and that prices were also high enough to have, under other circumstances, caused such an extension; but there is at present an impassable limit to the extension of this culture, and that is the possibility of cleaning the wool from the seed. The whole available population in the cotton districts, I believe to be now employed on this work, and that but for the introduction of the saw gin, even the extension shewn in my table could not have taken place. With the native machines, the foot roller and the churka, the present population is not equal to cleaning a larger crop of cotton than is now grown, and hence the importance of more efficient machines. The natives here are quite sensible of this, and in consequence the saw gin is rapidly coming into use. There are sixty and more I believe, costing from 50 to 200 rupees each, now at work in this Collectorate, and all the property of natives, who work them without assistance from Government, further than occasional visits from an Inspector, to see that they are in proper order. The demand for these machines is steadily increasing, for the cleaning of the native as well as the New Orleans crop, and the Government manufactory here has difficulty in supplying them fast enough. This is another cheering evidence of progress, and of the greater versatility and intelligence of the people here.

——— was quite right in imagining that a good deal of the cultivation in Tasgaon under native management was the result of *actual compulsion*. It is so in *all* native states and jagheers that I have seen. But you must not suppose that compulsion or any other process would enable the ryots to pay the enormous rates per beega, 2 to 10 rupees, which he mentions. These rates were *never* paid unless in a season of extraordinary abundance, but the native plan is to keep an impossible rate, in order to be enabled in good seasons to sweep the whole surplus into the exchequer. In Tasgaon I find from my notes made on the spot, that it was usual to collect under the native management only from ¼ to ½ of the full rates, and to lease out land besides, at low fixed rates, though not upon written engagements. But our authorities as usual overlooked these practical adjustments, and, to the great astonishment and dismay of the people, demanded payment of the full rates, and regarded their assertions that such a thing had never been heard of before, as attempts at imposition. The result was that a large extent of land was immediately thrown out of cultivation, but the Survey will luckily step in next year, and put matters to rights.

You will perceive from this, that, in spite of their enormous assessment, the Tasgaon ryots were not so badly off under the native system. They were slaves it is true; but their masters were considerate, and seldom tightened their bonds beyond the limits of endurance. They were not allowed to become too wealthy, but on the other hand never or seldom reduced below the level of a tolerable subsistence. They were the milch cows of the Jagheerdar, which, however, he took care should be milked by no one but himself. Accomplished extracters of the last drop, of the Marwarree and other kinds, so abundant in our districts, were not allowed to finger the udder at all in Tasgaon.

The gross produce in a well managed native district is certainly greater than in our unsurveyed districts, for which the unbending rules of our system of revenue management are very ill suited, but *far short* I should say of the gross produce of our surveyed districts where the settlement has been in operation for a few years, or long enough to teach the cultivator the advantages of liberty, and that he really now labours for himself, and not merely for the State. The peasantry under the survey settlements quickly acquire a certain degree of independence, but ages of freedom will be required to purge them thoroughly of the mean vices of slavery, —fraud, lying, and selfishness.—Your's very sincerely,

---

We may add, that, on looking into the latest reports from the Collector and the Revenue Commissioner, we find, among many statements very similar to those supplied in our correspondent's letter, a table shewing the increase of cultivation during the last seven years *for the whole Collectorate.* There has been no reaction during any part of this period: each year shewing a considerable advance on the one preceding it, and the first and last items of the statement are,

1844-45......................570,319 acres.

1850-51......................917,818 acres.

We extract also the following very interesting statements from the same report. The Collector, it is to be observed, had newly taken charge of the Zillah:—

"I have to state that I have been much struck with the generally prosperous condition of the cultivators, and with the absence of many of those signs of depression so remarkable in many provinces of this Presidency. One of these, particularly observable, is the independence of the ryots, who appear here for the most part to be free from the thraldom of Marwarees and other petty traders, which is so manifestly injurious in most parts of the Deccan* * * * *. It is not uncommon for the members of other than the agricultural classes to embark their capital in the improvement of extensive holdings, by the employment of hired labour."

CONCLUDING ARTICLE.

"There would be no want of pupils of the highest class for such institutions (model farms for educational purposes) did land *owners* learn practical agriculture. The expectant land-owner should undergo tuition in his profession. To acquire a knowledge of the duties of a landlord, he considers it unnecessary to undergo initiatory tuition. He conceives that these duties may be learned at any time, and seems to forget that the conducting a landed estate is a profession as difficult of thorough attainment as soldiership or legal lore. It strikes every one as an incongruity that a country gentleman should be unacquainted with country affairs. Is it not strange that he should require inducements to learn his hereditary profession, to become familiar with the only business which can enable him to enhance the value of his estate and increase his income?"—*Stephens' Book of the Farm.*

In concluding this series of articles, which it is proposed now to collect and publish in the form of a pamphlet, it will be well perhaps to state briefly what have been the writer's sources of information, and also to gather up, from the nine articles over which they are scattered, the chief results to which his inquiries have led him.

He has in the first place to confess his obligations to the Revenue Survey Commissioner for the unwearied kindness with which his numerous, minute, and perhaps, in some cases, almost unnecessarily cautious and sceptical inquiries, have been replied to, and for the stores of valuable information placed at his disposal in the Revenue Survey department.

He has also to thank the present Revenue Secretary for the liberality which has allowed the most ample access —not to favourable specimens merely, or select portions but—to the whole of the revenue records relating to the subject in the Government archives. And he wishes to record his very high admiration of the perfect candour with which the inquiries he has presumed to make in this department have been answered; of the willingness, so evident, that every part of the subject should, to the full extent of the writer's capabilities for his self-imposed task, be thoroughly sifted and examined; and of the scrupulous anxiety to abstain, while yet supplying every requisite elucidation, from the suggestion of any *inference* from the evidence, leaving it in every case to produce its legitimate effect on the mind of the inquirer.

He is bound, too, after reading some twenty volumes of revenue records, containing every thing connected with the revenues of the Deccan Collectorates for the last four or five years, to state that the liberality with which the survey settlement has been planned and carried out, pervades the whole of the correspondence and orders of the Government on the subject of revenue generally. In no instance where a low assessment has been proposed, or where large remissions have been granted, as in unsurveyed districts they frequently must be, has he met with a single phrase implying that the Government looked wistfully or regretfully at the abandoned revenue.

The response, wherever it proceeds beyond the expression of a simple sanction, is invariably either a hope on the part of the Government that the remissions have been sufficiently liberal, or an expression of apprehension lest they should not have been so. It occurs occasionally that two Revenue Officers differ about the amount of remissions to be granted, and the writer has been struck by the fact in every case of this kind which he has met with, it is the more liberal officer whose opinions have been adopted by the Government—and this, although he may even be the junior and subordinate one,—considerations of discipline or of the propriety of maintaining authority, having apparently no influence on the decision whenever it is a question of the possibility of an oppressive collection.

On the other hand there are proofs enough in these records that the whole system of revenue management is susceptible of many improvements. Very evidently it is never made sufficiently a profession. This is a conviction which grows upon us the more, the further we read. Whatever Persian or Sanscrit we might sacrifice in their attainment, we should certainly insist, as the qualifications for a Collectorship, or for any other revenue appointment, on a first rate course of scientific agriculture in one of our agricultural schools at home, and a thorough acquaintance with one or two of the best writers on political economy.

The more we read of these reports the more impressed are we with the conviction that we have in them the productions of gentlemen, fairly educated, and for the most part thoroughly well-intentioned, but whose chances of usefulness to the country would be greatly increased were they educated with much closer reference to their future employment, and taught to consider it a profession requiring the same attention from them which a lawyer pays to his cases, or a physician to his pathology and his practice of medicine.

Another defect which we fancy we perceive is, that the whole internal Government of the Civil Service is too lax. The gravest errors—errors which bring, for instance, temporary ruin upon a whole district—are visited with nothing more serious than a few expostulatory sentences—a little of Carlyle's "articulate wind." Now, depreciatory words, when they fix the estimation in which a man shall be held, and when he feels that upon this estimation depend probably all his prospects in life, are grave matters enough. But our Civilian is perfectly well assured that nothing said on these occasions will either interfere with his promotion, or even become public enough to affect his reputation. It is only, so to speak, his elder brother who is temporarily annoyed at his conduct, and who professes to be, and perhaps is exceedingly angry; but who, as the culprit well knows, will never dream of excluding him from his appointed share of their common patrimony.

We think, too, that we can perceive, that it is by no means on all occasions sufficient that the most experienced and the ablest men in the service should recommend a particular regulation; that the government should be convinced of its importance, and that it should be formally enacted and ordered to have the force of law. An individual revenue officer will still, it would seem, consider that he is entitled to treat such a regulation as an open question, and to enforce it or not, according to his own estimate of its propriety. An old established piece of revenue management was, to place a guard over the crops when harvested, and allow them to be removed from the village only upon payment of the revenue. The wretched ryot who could not possibly pay his rent from his own resources, unless by selling his crop, and who could not sell it, as he was not allowed to carry it to market, had evidently therefore no alternative but to resort to the money lender. All this under the new settlement has been changed,—or at least the regulations which are to change it have been formally enacted and promulgated. The ryot is made entire master of his field, and of everything which he may grow in it; and the periods of payment—the *quarter days*—have been fixed for much later dates,—dates so late as to afford him the most ample time to carry his produce to the market, and make a deliberate and *bona fide* sale of it.

But one overzealous revenue officer, struck with the extreme folly of the government in thus abandoning its hold on the crop, refuses altogether to be a party to anything so suicidal; and, long after the most ample experience in other districts has shewn that the new policy is attended by no kind of danger to the revenue, persists in the old style of management, and is with some difficulty reduced to a reluctant and tardy obedience. Several seasons, too, are found necessary to teach others that such a regulation has really been sanctioned, and that the government is in earnest when it proposes to have it carried into execution.

One remedy probably for a great deal of this is, increased publicity. Experiments are made, and succeed or fail, as the case may be, without becoming sufficiently public to attract the attention of any, even of the government's own officers, beyond the two or three who may happen to be actually engaged in them. Not only is the general public allowed to remain a good deal in the dark, but even the service itself would seem to be sometimes very badly informed on important matters closely perhaps connected with its official duties. We are happy to see many indications of a change in this respect. The government has, we are quite convinced, very much to gain from publicity and exceedingly little to fear ; and this is an opinion which we see is gaining ground among the most intelligent and the best informed of its members. We can very honestly say for ourselves that access to the records has, on the whole, raised our opinion of the general management in the department we have been studying, The cases of incompetence, or blundering inattention, are neither graver nor more numerous than we were fully prepared to meet with, while the uniform liberality of feeling which pervades whatever emanates from the government on the subject of revenue, has certainly to some extent taken us by surprise.

In conclusion, the results of the new revenue arrangements in the Deccan up to the present time are, we conceive, the following :—

1st. The reduced rates appear almost every where to be followed by a rush on the land, and far more land is taken up than the ryots have properly capital for, leading, as a necessary consequence, to a great deal of very slovenly cultivation.

2nd. There occurs subsequently, in almost every instance, a period of reaction. Cultivation carried on without sufficient capital exhausts the soil, and a time usually arrives when the lands reported in the annual revenue returns as thrown up during the year from "poverty and exhaustion," that is to say from the poverty of the ryots and the exhaustion of the soil, to which may perhaps be added, though this is less certain, from the discouragement arising from glutted markets, exceeds the new land taken into cultivation during the same year.

3rd. This reaction—this unfavourable balance of lands thrown up over new lands—taken into cultivation, is in no case very important in amount. The gross produce in spite of the imperfect tillage being, from the greater breadth of land under cultivation, decidedly greater, agricultural capital does every where on the whole increase as do also, although (except perhaps in Dharwar,) very much more slowly than could be wished, the exports which are to relieve the overstocked markets.

4th. In the best districts some improvement is perceptible in the style of agriculture, and in the implements in use among the people, the result of increased means, and of an increase of independent feeling and energy on the part of the ryot. We have already noticed the successful introduction of New Orleans Cotton, and of a modification of the American Saw Gin; and we may here add to them the rapidly increasing number of convenient light two-wheeled bullock carts—a conveyance introduced into these provinces by our revenue officers. The only Collectorate from which we have been able to obtain returns under this head, is the Sholapore one; and for that district the statement is as follows:—

1834-35, Number of carts in the district 430
1846.. 1,907
By last returns.. 2,643

Also in Kurmulla, a talooka previously included in the Nugger Collectorate, but now combined with Sholapore:

1846.. 391
By last returns.. 983

5th. There is on the other hand everywhere a lamentable amount of indebtedness, and of a thraldom to money lenders most depressing in its effects on the ryots' energies. But this again is certainly diminishing in the best districts, and perhaps also very slowly in the others.

6. Although whoever set himself to look for pauperism and misery in the province, may find quite enough of them to excite the most painful feelings in him; and although the five shillings an acre of returns from the land, and the shilling or fifteen-pence of rent, tell a most sorrowful tale of wretched un-skill, un-energy, and unproductiveness generally, and cry aloud to us to do whatever may be in our power to increase the intelligence

and to raise the industrial character of the people ; yet, leaving individual cases, and perhaps peculiarly unfortunate talookas, and looking to the result in the mass, there are certainly quite unmistakeable indications to the effect that the tide is slowly turning. We have already stated many of these, and will only here refer our readers again to the rapidly increasing exports and imports, and especially to the large and growing absorption of silver and copper, a fact which can only, we believe, be explained by supposing that in some of our districts silver ornaments and copper vessels, the indisputable signs of growing prosperity in a Hindu community, are decidedly on the increase.

We have now arrived at the end of our inquiry, reserving some attempts at a history of prices which we have prepared, for an Appendix. We have striven above all things to be perfectly truthful throughout, to the utmost of our ability. Admiring greatly as we do the liberal feeling, the sound principles, and the skill and energy which have been brought to bear upon the new settlement, we have certainly greatly *desired* to find that the promoters of it had met with their reward in the increased and increasing prosperity of the districts into which it has been introduced. But we have been at least equally anxious that our wishes should have no influence on our judgment ; and we must so far risk incurring the charge of want of modesty as to state, that we are satisfied, that on the whole, we have succeeded in depicting the Survey Settlement and its results, and the general condition of the Ryots in the Deccan, as they really are.

APPENDIX.

No. I.

The correspondent, a letter from whom we inserted in No. IX., has sent us a few remarks on our concluding article, or, rather, on the six paragraphs of it in which we have summed up the results of our inquiries.

Our correspondent thinks that we have scarcely done justice to the results of the new settlement. We believe that we have come to the only conclusions which the evidence—furnished chiefly by the Government records—will warrant.

We also think that some of his remarks are hardly so much comments on our statements as anxious attempts to guard against possible misconstructions of them. But even so considered, the criticisms may be useful, and we therefore insert them in an Appendix.

"Before venturing any observations on your summing up, I must premise that you have had before you a great deal of correspondence on the subject of the settlement, which I have never seen at all, and that my remarks, therefore, will have reference to that portion only of the evidence of which I am cognizant.

"I am quite at one with your other critics as to the perfect fairness of your whole representation, and your summing up agrees in the main with my own views, though considerably less favourable to the Survey. The following suggestions will explain the points on which I am at all doubtful of the validity of your results. I will take your six paragraphs in order.

"1st.—The deficiency of capital may have been compensated by increased industry, and the evidence seems to shew that it was so to a considerable extent. The slovenly cultivation referred to under this head, is not, I think, proved, unless it refer to the new land taken into cultivation immediately following the introduction of the new settlement.

"2nd.—I am not satisfied that cultivation carried on without sufficient capital exhausts the soil. It is not in my opinion the want of capital so much as a bad style of farming that exhausts the land. It is continued cropping without manure that does the evil, and the greater the capital employed in this style of farming, the more rapidly will the exhaustion proceed, because the heavier will be the crops taken off without anything being given to the soil in return.

"3rd.—The remarks on 1st paragraph apply with greater force to this. I am not aware of anything in the evidence that supports the conclusion that, *after the reaction*, the land in cultivation is more imperfectly tilled than before the settlement. This is a point to be established by testimony more than by statistics. Frere's account of Indapoor and my own observation, if not overbalanced by the evidence of equally competent witnesses, lead, I think, to the conclusion that improved tillage is a general result of the survey settlements, and consequently that a gross produce has been increased by this, as well as by extension of cultivation. A further inference from this would be, that agricultural capital increases not slowly but rapidly. Without having seen your appendix on prices, I am not in a position to offer an opinion on your conclusion that the markets are overstocked. Prices in this country are ultimately dependent on the necessity of exporting enough to meet our home charges, and this will probably always keep them at a low standard.

"4th.—The remarks on the improvements in tillage already given, apply also here. I may as well mention in this place, that I greatly understated the number of saw gins sold to natives in this Collectorate, [Dharwar] in a former letter. I have now obtained from Mr. Blount, the superintendent of cotton experiments in this province, the following information as to the number, size and price of gins sold in this Collectorate up to the present time, which may be relied on as correct.

Number of Gins sold.	Number of Saws in each Gin.	Price of each Gin—Rs.	Price of the whole—Rs.	
1	25	225	225	All purchased by Natives.
2	24	225	450	
3	20	220	660	
48	18	200	9600	
9	14	170	1530	
3	13	170	510	
5	10	100	500	
1	8	80	80	
115	7	50	5750	
187			19,305	

5 Purchased by European dealers.

192 Total number sold up to this time.

"The first sales were made in 1848, so that in four years the cotton dealers of this Collectorate have invested 20,000 rupees in the purchase of these machines. This is, I think, a fact worth recording, and I wish you could manage to substitute it for the former incorrect allusion to the number sold.

"5th.—I agree entirely with you in regard to this head. Have you noticed a sad illustration of its correctness in a report published in the *Bombay Gazette* of 6th instant, of a village money-lender in the Sholapoor Collectorate having been murdered by some of his debtors, under circumstances that give strong grounds for suspecting that the whole body of villagers approved of the deed? This casual withdrawal of the curtain for a moment discloses a state of things quite appalling, if we consider the case, as it is to be feared we must, as a result of the general relations which our administration of civil justice has brought about between debtor and creditor in agricultural villages.

"6th.—I question the propriety of the use of the word Pauperism in the paragraph, and doubt if any enquiry would discover anywhere in the surveyed district the existence of what is termed Pauperism in Europe. I understand the word to refer to a state of things in which the able-bodied and willing to work can find no work, and would starve but for the aid of others. I cannot recollect having ever met with this in any of the surveyed districts, and should say that Pauperism is unknown in them all. Pauper cultivators in the phraseology of revenue reports are to be met with, but these are bankrupt farmers, and they would have no difficulty in finding work as labourers. If you refer to the latter, it would be desirable, I think, to explain the sense in which you use the word.

"With these few reservations your conclusions seem to me to be as sound, as the whole tone of your review is eminently fair and impartial."

Having inserted these remarks, we ought perhaps to give specimens of a great deal of testimony which we have—especially from native correspondents—differing very widely from this letter. We fear, however, that we are already too voluminous, and will only say that in the very few places in which the difference between ourselves and our correspondent is not merely an apparent or verbal one, we find ourselves compelled to think him somewhat too sanguine in his views; and that, after the fullest consideration of all the evidence we have been able to collect on the subject, we adhere deliberately to the conclusions contained in our final article.

APPENDIX II.

The subjoined Tables A. and B. have been compiled, with the exception of the column of "Present prices," partly from the records of the Peshwa's Government, and partly from old family papers in the possession of a native gentleman, Trimbuk Hari Vurtuk.

(A)

AVERAGE MARKET PRICES OF DIFFERENT COMMODITIES AT POONAH.

QUANTITY PER RUPEE.

From the year 1775 to 1781.

Names of Commodities.	1775 *Pylees	1775 Shairs	1776 P.	1776 S.	1777 P.	1777 S.	1778 P.	1778 S.	1779 P.	1779 S.	1780 P.	1780 S.	1781 P.	1781 S.
Bajree	5	3	1	3	0	0	7	0	5	1	4	2	6	0
Jowaree	6	2	1	3	7	0	7	2	5	1	6	3	6	2
Rice	0	0	1	0	0	0	3	3	3	1½	3	2	0	0
Wheat	5	1	1	3	4	1	5	1	5	2	0	0	0	0
Till	3	0		0	0	0	3	2	0	0	0	0	3	1
Gram	4	1		2	4	1	4	3	4	2	4	½	5	0
Common Salt	0	0		0	0	0	10	0	7	0	10	0	6	1
Gram, split and husked	0	0	1	0	0	0	0	0	0	0	3	2	0	0
Toory ditto	0	0	1	0	0	0	0	0	4	3	4	0	5	0
Mustard Seed	0	0	1	0	0	0	4	0	0	0	3	2	0	0

From 1794 to 1804.

Names of Commodities.	1794 P.	1794 S.	1795 P.	1795 S.	1796 P.	1796 S.	1797 P.	1797 S.	1798 P.	1798 S.	1799 P.	1799 S.	1800 P.	1800 S.	1801 P.	1801 S.	1802 P.	1802 S.	1803 P.	1803 S.	1804 P.	1804 S.
Bajree	2	0	0	0	3	0	2	2	3	1	0	0	4	0	5	0	3	2	2	0	3	1
Jowaree	0	0	4	1	3	0	3	0	3	0	3	1	3	1	4	2	3	2	1	3	4	1
Rice	0	0	2	1	0	0	0	0	3	1	2	2	2	2	2	2	2	2	1	1	0	0
Wheat	2	0	2	3	2	0	2	1	3	0	2	2	2	1	2	2	3	1	1	3	0	0
Till	3	0	0	0	0	0	1	1	0	0	1	2	0	0	0	0	0	0	2	0	0	0
Gram	1	3	0	0	2	1½	2	½	3	1	0	0	0	0	3	3	4	2	0	0	3	0
Common Salt	7	2	0	0	0	0	6	1	0	0	0	0	7	0	3	2	6	1	4	0	0	0
Gram, split and husked	0	0	0	0	0	0	1	3	3	2	2	1	2	0	2	2	0	0	1	½	2	0
Toory ditto	3	0	0	0	0	0	2	3	2	½	2	1	2	0	3	3	0	0	1	1	0	0
Mustard Seed	6	0	2	1	0	0	0	0	2	3	0	0	2	2	3	0	0	0	2	0	0	0

From 1817 (excepting 1820 and 1824) to 1828. Present rates, 1852. Averages.

Names of Commodities.	1817 P.	1817 S.	1818 P.	1818 S.	1819 P.	1819 S.	1821 P.	1821 S.	1822 P.	1822 S.	1823 P.	1823 S.	1825 P.	1825 S.	1826 P.	1826 S.	1827 P.	1827 S.	1828 P.	1828 S.	Present rates 1852 P.	Present rates 1852 S.	Average rates for 7 years from 1775 to 1781. Pylees.	Average rates for 11 years from 1794 to 1804. Pylees.	Average rates for 10 years from 1817 to 1828 save 1820 & 1824. Pylees.
Bajree	4	0	3	2	2	3	5	2	6	0		2	3	0	6	0	5	2	4	2	6	2	5.71	3.167	4.98
Jowaree	4	3	3	3	2	3	4	2	10	0		2	4	1	5	2	6	0	8	0	8	2	6.73	3.575	5.68
Rice	2	2	0	0	0	0	3	2	3	2		0	3	0	4	0	4	3	4	0	3	2	2.4	2.21	3.7
Wheat	3	1	3	0	3	1	2	1	5	1		1	3	3	3	3	3	3	4	3	5	2	4.35	2.525	2.57
Till	0	0	2	0	2	0	0	0	2	0		0	1	0	3	0	2	2	2	2	4	0	3.25	1.69	2.55
Gram	4	1	0	0	0	0	0	0	4	2		0	4	0	0	0	0	0	0	0	5	1	4.46	2.86	4.5
Common Salt	7	0	9	1	10	0	10	2	3	0		0	7	1	3	0	10	0	10	0	6	2	8.81	4.75	9.73
Gram, split and husked	3	0	2	2	2	2	3	0	4	0		0	2	3	3	0	4	0	4	0	4	2	3.5	2.018	3.15
Toory ditto	0	0	1	3	1	3	3	0	0	0		2	2	1	0	0	4	0	5	0	4	3	4.58	2.16	3.31
Mustard Seed	0	0	3	0	0	0	0	0	3	0	2	5	3	0	2	0	0	0	2	0	4	3	3.73	3.04	1.61

* 4 Shairs or 8 Seers make one Pylee.

(B)

AVERAGE MARKET PRICES OF DIFFERENT ARTICLES AT POONAH.

QUANTITY PER RUPEE.

From the year 1775 to 1781.

Names of Articles.	1775 *Shairs	1775 Q'ters.	1776 S.	1776 Q.	1777 S.	1777 Q.	1778 S.	1778 Q.	1779 S.	1779 Q.	1780 S.	1780 Q.	1781 S.	1781 Q.
Sugar	3	2	2	3	3	0	2	3	0	0	0	0	3	0
Sugar Candy	1	1	1	½	1	2	1	3	0	0	0	0	1	1
Ghee	1	3½	2	1	2	½	1	2½	2	1	0	0	0	0
Goor	5	0	6	0	7	1	9	0	0	0	0	0	5	3
Oil	5	2	4	2	4	3	5	2	5	3	0	0	5	0
Betel Nut	0	0	2	3	2	1½	2	2	0	3	0	0	2	2
Cocoa-nut kernel	0	0	3	0	3	0	2	3	0	0	0	0	3	1
Turmeric	5	0	6	0	6	3	10	0	0	0	0	0	5	0
Milk	0	0	10	2	8	2	0	0	7	0	0	0	9	2

From 1794 to 1804.

Names of Articles.	1794 S.	1794 Q.	1795 S.	1795 Q.	1796 S.	1796 Q.	1797 S.	1797 Q.	1798 S.	1798 Q.	1799 S.	1799 Q.	1800 S.	1800 Q.	1801 S.	1801 Q.	1802 S.	1802 Q.	1803 S.	1803 Q.	1804 S.	1804 Q.
Sugar	2	2	2	2	0	0	2	½	2	0	2	1	2	1	2	2	3	0	2	3	0	0
Sugar Candy	1	1½	0	0	0	0	0	0	1	1	1	1	0	0	1	1	0	0	0	0	0	0
Ghee	1	3	1	3	1	2	1	1½	1	3	1	½	1	2	1	2	2	0	1	0	1	3
Goor	3	3	0	0	0	0	4	1½	4	0	5	2	4	2	3	2	6	0	5	2	0	0
Oil	3	1½	3	1	0	0	3	1	3	2	4	0	4	2	3	3	5	1	3	3	3	2
Betel Nut	3	1	0	0	0	0	3	0	2	2	2	0	0	0	2	1	2	3	2	2	0	0
Cocoa-nut kernel	2	3	0	0	0	0	0	0	4	0	4	2	1	2	3	0	0	0	6	2	0	0
Turmeric	3	½	3	3	3	0	3	3	4	2	0	0	5	1	5	1	5	0	3	1	0	0
Milk	0	0	9	1	0	0	7	0	9	1	10	0	10	3	10	0	12	0	12	0	0	0

From 1817 to 1828, excepting 1820 and 1824. Present rates, 1852. Averages.

Names of Articles.	1817 S.	1817 Q.	1818 S.	1818 Q.	1819 S.	1819 Q.	1821 S.	1821 Q.	1822 S.	1822 Q.	1823 S.	1823 Q.	1825 S.	1825 Q.	1826 S.	1826 Q.	1827 S.	1827 Q.	1828 S.	1828 Q.	Present rates 1852 S.	Present rates 1852 Q.	Average rates for 7 years, from 1775 to 1781. Shairs.	Average rates for 11 years from 1794 to 1804. Shairs.	Average rates for 10 years, from 1817 to 1828 save 1820 and 1824. Shairs.
Sugar	2	2	2	3	3	0	2	1	0	0	2	1½	3	1	0	0	0	0	2	1	4	2	3	2.44	2.492
Sugar Candy	0	0	0	0	0	0	1	2	2	0	1	1	1	3	2	0	1	3	1	2	3	0	1.35	1.27	1.089
Ghee	1	2	1	2	2	0	1	½	1	3	2	1	1	1	2	2	2	1	2	0	3	0	2	1.545	1.767
Goor	4	2	5	1	5	0	5	1	5	1	6	1	4	2	5	2	4	1	6	0	8	0	6.6	4.5	5.15
Oil	3	2	4	0	3	2	3	3	2	2	4	0	2	3	4	0	4	1	5	0	7	1	5.18	3.713	3.825
Betel Nut	0	0	0	0	0	0	0	0	0	0	0	0	0	0	0	0	0	0	0	0	4	2	2.5	2.007	0
Cocoa-nut kernel	5	3	4	1	4	1	5	0	4	0	4	0	4	1	4	0	5	0	5	0	6	2	3	3.708	4.283
Turmeric	6	0	6	0	5	2	12	0	3	3	3	3	3	3	4	0	5	2	3	0	14	0	6.5	4.037	4.725
Milk	9	0	12	0	9	0	9	0	12	0	11	0	10	0	16	0	11	0	13	0	18	0	8.9	10.08	11.2

* 2 Seers = 1 Shair.

(B.)

AVERAGE RATES OF WAGES AT POONAH.

From 1775 to 1804.

Labourers.	Monthly wages. Rs.	A.
Cook.........	4	...
Water bearer......	4	...
Carpenter	10	...
Servant...	4	...
Female servant...	2	8
Labourer	3	12
Female labourer ..	2	12
Boy	1	12
Bricklayer..........	10	...
Stone-cutter... ...	15	...
Palanquin bearer.	6	...
Servant under Carpenter.........	7	8

This table is framed from the old records of family expenditure of a private gentleman, named Trimbuck Hurri Vurtuck.

From 1798 to 1820.

Labourers.	Monthly wages. Rs.	A.
Carpenter No. 1......	15	...
ditto No. 2......	12	...
ditto No. 3......	10	...
Bricklayer	15	...
ditto No. 2.....	12	...
ditto „ 3 ...	10	...
Servant...	5	10
Female servant	3	8
Boy...	3	...
Tailor 1st rate	15	...
Hired Pony with a driver	15	...
ditto Bullock ditto....	6	...
do. Cart do... .	15	...
Sawyer..	15	...

This is taken from the Nirukh papers of the Peshwa's Dufter.

Of 1852.

Labourers.	Monthly wages. Rs.	A.
Carpenter 1st	15	...
ditto 2nd	12	...
ditto 3rd	10	...
Bricklayer	15	...
ditto No. 2	12	...
ditto „ 3	10	...
Servant...	3	8
Female servant .	2	8
Labourer.	3	12
Woman...	2	13
Boy...	2	13
Tailor 1st rate	15	...
Stone cutter..	15	...
Sawyer...	16	...
Hired Pony with a driver...	10	...
ditto Cart do.	16	...

The table C. has been furnished by some native friends, grain dealers in Poonah.

(C.)

AVERAGE RATES at Poonah of Bajree and Joaree, the grains most largely consumed in the Deccan (and in Guzerat,) from the year 1837 to 1852. Quantity per rupee in pylees and shairs.

Bajree.						Joaree.					
Year.	Rates. P.	S.	Year.	Rates. P.	S.	Year.	Rates. P.	S.	Year.	Rates. P.	S.
1837	6	3	1845	5	0	1837	8	0	1845	6	0
1838	8	0	1846	3	1½	1838	11	1½	1846	3	3
1839	5	¾	1847	6	0	1839	5	0	1847	6	2½
1840	6	3	1848	10	1½	1840	8	0	1848	12	3
1841	7	0	1849	9	2	1841	9	1	1849	12	0
1842	7	1	1850	6	0	1842	9	3	1850	6	2
1843	8	1	1851	5	3	1843	9	3	1851	7	0
1844	7	2	1852	6	2	1844	8	0	1852	9	0

			Pylees.
Bajree average for	1st eight	years.	7,086
Do. do.	2nd do.	do.	6,560

Joaree average for	1st eight	years.	8,640
Do. do.	2nd do.	do.	7,953

In the second eight years, one (1846) of very unusual drought occurs;—omitting this, the second averages would be Bajree 7 pylees, Joaree 8.55,—almost identical with the averages for the first eight years.

The general results are of considerable interest and importance. It will be seen that,—

1st. General prices now *are not half what they were at the commencement of the century!* and that the change has been entirely consequent on our accession to power in the Deccan.

2nd. That the fall has long since ceased, and that prices now are either stationary, or, perhaps, slightly tending to rise.

3rd. That the prices of labour have remained wonderfully constant for upwards of three quarters of a century, in spite of great fluctuations, and even great permanent changes in the prices of food; custom, the regulator of so many things in India, although powerless over the prices of commodities, yet ruling the labour market almost absolutely,—as it does, with us in England, the fees of lawyers and physicians.

If we now ask whether we are to rejoice or lament over this low range of prices, the answer will depend very much on the class of interest with which we happen to sympathize. Low prices of produce, of course, necessitate low rates on the land, and the Government, and the native aristocracy, who share the rent with the Government, have to content themselves with a much lower money revenue.

The importance of this will depend on the extent to which the revenue consuming classes expend their incomes on foreign commodities. As prices are low, the low money incomes—did the consumers demand only the produce of the country—would be just as effective as the former high ones had been. Our Government, however, and, even the native aristocracy of the present day, are very large consumers of foreign goods, and the low rates, therefore, represent to them a real and very great impoverishment of the province. On the other hand, the labourer who obtains the same wages as formerly, and spends almost the whole of them on the produce of the country, which produce is at half its former price, is of course virtually twice as rich. And, indeed, the general result of our *regime* is the elevation of the lower classes, and the depression of the higher. A Dufterdar, the chief native revenue officer in a province, and a village low caste watchman, although still greatly different in social estimation, are, under our levelling rule, undoubtedly much more nearly on an equality than they ever were before. Our Government is emphatically the friend of the poor, and the deadly enemy—not of a commercial or manufacturing aristocracy, whenever that shall arise—but of the old land-revenue-consuming, fighting, and ruling aristocracy.

It will be proper to notice that a part—doubtless much the smaller part—of the reduction of prices, is the result of the abolition of transit duties, the penetration (as far as it has proceeded) of the Deccan by cart-roads, and the greater general security which now exists ; and that, so far, the fall of prices is an unmixed benefit, cheapening goods for all, and reducing nobody's income. Also that, simultaneously with the fall of prices here, the progress of commerce and industry abroad, since the great European pacification of 1815, and especially of English commerce and industry, has caused a very great reduction in the cost of many kinds of foreign goods, rendering the diminution of the money revenue of the province—a diminution which we have seen is only important with reference to foreign products—less felt than it otherwise would be.

And finally we may observe that, as far as we can judge from only one of the Deccan markets, the Revenue Survey Settlement, with all the increased cultivation to which it gives rise, has not produced any general decline of prices, the present very low range having been reached, apparently, from fifteen to twenty years ago. We must certainly add, however, that this very interesting question is precisely the one concerning which we are in possession of the least amount of information.

THE END.